CW00507460

"I've been working with de(
fifty years. The picture pai.
too recognisable. I've bee
fictional ones the pages of .... This is a
very practical book. It understands the issues and
represents an invaluable resource for those who are
seeking to work with churches to 'turn the tide.'
Effective leadership is undoubtedly key in making a
difference, but even good leaders need resources to
help them along the way. Turning the Tide represents just
such a resource for those leaders with the calling,
commitment and courage to engage in this crucial task."
Revd Dr Martin Robinson
Fellowship of Churches of Christ

"Canon Phil has experienced years of combining the
leading of the Holy Spirit with practical applications in
maintaining and growing a local church.
This book addresses issues that normally appear in
conferences and training seminars. Phil and Brian,
however, bring a modern parable and uniquely appeal
not just to leaders, but to all who wish to see their church
become effective in their community.
If Jesus could fill a boat with fish, what could He do in our
community if we understood how to cast our net?
This book looks at the practical and spiritual applications
required in order to become relevant."
Rt Revd Dr David E Carr OBE OSL EKHC

"Phil and Brian bring their many years of experience and passion together in this innovative resource. Their desire to see the church grow and people enter into a life-transforming relationship with Jesus Christ oozes through every page. Through this book you'll find deep wisdom from those who have trod the path before you and bear not only the scars but the joy of seeing God's kingdom grow.

I love the way that Phil and Brian weave us through the experiences of the Questor family as they explore both faith and church. The experiences encountered are ones that happen in local churches every Sunday across this nation and maybe in yours.

There are important lessons drawn out from each encounter that any church leader, church planter or church leadership team would do well to take heed of. This isn't just an informative read, but is a very practical resource, with lots of ideas you can put into practice that could affect change in any local church context. It also offers a helpful discussion section for local churches that can assist in examining each context carefully and initiate changes that will facilitate growth.

I wholeheartedly recommend this as a part of any church planter's or church leader's tool kit. Don't begin the adventure without it."

Revd Ashley Cooper
Principal of Cliff College

"In a time when we're told that church attendance is dropping, it's important for the church to take a look at itself and ask difficult questions. At UCB we believe that a brand new, exciting move of God is coming that will be so big, the churches will struggle to contain it. The question is, if this happened tomorrow, would your church be able to cope?

Turning the Tide is a frank and honest look at some of the practices and behaviours of some of our churches. From peeling noticeboards to stewed tea and unfriendly cliques, the book covers it all and asks challenging questions while also providing some very practical solutions. If you're in church ministry and longing to see your church grow and also be 'fighting fit' and ready for a great move of God, Phil and Brian have many years of collective pastoral experience to share."

David L'Herroux
Chief Executive, United Christian Broadcasters

"Brian and Phil offer simple and practical guidelines gleaned over forty years that will aid and assist all those seeking to address decline in church attendance and to play their part in 'turning the tide.' I highly recommend them, the work they've pioneered and this book."

Canon Billy Kennedy
International Leader, Pioneer Network

TURNING THE TIDE

Building a new future

for the church

Thanks

Thank you to our family and very many friends who over the years have shared their experience and have worked tirelessly with us to communicate the Good News in relevant and contemporary ways.

Contents

PHILIP BARBER AND BRIAN BARBER

Foreword

In the opening words of Turning the Tide, Brian and Phil Barber state that the driving force behind the book is a combination of "faith in Jesus, passion to see His Kingdom grow and deep concern for His Church."

These interwoven realities have been consistently articulated – and demonstrated – by Brian and Phil in the forty years that I've known them. For many years, they've lived this out, first at Swan Bank Church, Burslem, and, for the last thirty years, at Potters' Church in Birches Head. Though their Christian life and leadership have found expression among and through the Methodist family in Stoke-on-Trent, both Brian's and Phil's influence extends to the wider Christian community. The stories they relate apply in any location. Their vision embraces God's Kingdom and the whole of the Christian Church.

Turning the Tide challenges us not to accept as fact that the decline in attendance being experienced by some churches is inevitable and irreversible. This in itself represents a change of mindset for those of us who have for a long time faced the ongoing challenges of decrease in church attendance and decline in corporate spiritual activities, together with an increase in the tensions of maintaining programmes, raising funds and repairing elderly church buildings.

Brian and Phil insist that by asking strategic questions, making significant decisions and taking practical steps, it's possible to reverse decline and enable growth. They lead us through scenarios based around public worship, church buildings, communication, church programmes, leadership styles and more – in each case analysing the issues, offering potential remedies and posing pertinent questions.

As the authors acknowledge, readers may be offended by the strong echoes of reality contained in their fictitious stories. They will certainly be challenged to face up to historic blind-spots, to correct long-held misperceptions and to gain new perspectives. But any personal affront that may arise will be the result of "the faithful wounds of a friend" (Proverbs 27:6), whose intention is to bring long-term benefit and blessing, even though the process may incur some pain in the short-term.

Readers also gain the opportunity of being impregnated with new hope, inspired by new possibilities and encouraged in new ways of "being" and "doing." Engaging with this book will, I believe, more than repay the effort involved. Read and be blessed!

Robert Mountford

Ecumenical Officer for Birmingham, the Black Country and Staffordshire

TURNING THE TIDE

Introduction

Faith in Jesus, passion to see His Kingdom grow, and deep concern for His Church – these are the driving forces that brought us together to write this book and they lie at the very heart of it. It's written from a background within Methodism, but we hope that it may be helpful to members of other denominations. So, we offer our ideas and thoughts for your careful consideration. Please use those that are appropriate to your own situation.

Does your church struggle to organise itself in a way that causes growth and life, and which is attractive to the unchurched majority? Do you sometimes wonder how you can more effectively grow a church if you are a member of the clergy or congregation? It's our belief that there are many **simple strategies** which can be employed to turn a culture of decline into one which provides hope and a future.

The Christian Church was of course **founded by Jesus** and is the community of God's people where anyone can find faith, enter into fellowship, learn to worship Him and grow as His disciples. It can be a great place to belong, but we're genuinely saddened by the failure of many churches to help others to find Him and so they find themselves in serious decline.

Our intention in these chapters is to help leaders and Christian people face difficult truths and find ways to help their churches grow. We all have "unknown unknowns" regarding our work and professional lives. Members of the clergy, church leaders, church council members (or their equivalent) and those who exercise particular ministries, paid or unpaid, in the churches to which they belong, are no different. If you are one, you may feel you have **significant gaps** in your understanding of how to grow church. It's even possible to be totally unaware that you as a leader or church member have never developed these skills. Maybe at the back of your mind there is a nagging thought that, despite all your sincere efforts, your church isn't growing and you really don't know what to do, so you have all been ploughing on, putting in a huge effort for very little return.

In John 21 it's recorded that Jesus appeared to some disciples on the beach of the Sea of Galilee. They had fished all night and **caught nothing**. They were experienced fishermen with, as they thought, great skill in locating and catching fish. Jesus simply told them to throw their net over the right side of the boat and when they did so, their net was full to bursting. This is very similar to the task of winning men, women, young people and children into God's Kingdom and thus growing the church. Lay and ordained leaders may believe they are very well trained and equipped yet despite their huge and sincere efforts very few human fish are caught, and, due to demographic decline, their church gradually shrinks. This can be deeply discouraging, though it is puzzling why so many in positions of responsibility persist with methods that are obviously not achieving good results.

Imagine a factory that persists with labour intensive production techniques while a rival invests in modern technology and produces the same goods far more cheaply. Surely the factory **would have to change**, even though to do so would require some painful decisions. Otherwise, it might go out of business. Our product – the Gospel – remains unchanging, but the methods we employ to communicate the Good News to people must surely change or we will go out of business too. Just like the disciples who were fishing, we need to change direction. The aim of this book is to expose and bring to light failed strategies and suggest practical ways that might be employed to achieve better results.

Which of us wouldn't want our church to grow when our primary task is to "go into all the world and **make disciples**?" We believe that, just as every seed has the potential within it for life, so churches should naturally grow. Where Gospel seeds are properly sown at the right time in the right soil and conditions, they will germinate and produce a harvest. However, growing church is a skill which requires the application of a complicated set of techniques depending on the target people group. There's no single method or idea which is the touchstone to church growth — variety and flexibility are required. Today's successful technique can quickly become obsolete in our fast-changing culture. We offer in this book a variety of possible situations with many different approaches to try. We have included in the text questions to help discussion so that churches can find their own way forward. We hope that you will find ideas appropriate to your own situation, and we sincerely wish you great success.

This book is, unusually, a mix of fiction, observation and suggestion. It's a **modern parable** – a fictional story from which truth can be understood. The fiction is provocative

– deliberately – not to be cruel or unkind but to provoke self-analysis and discussion and help church people see things from the perspective of someone who has rarely or never been to church before and who has little understanding of its theology, language or culture. We've tried to adopt Jesus' main teaching style which was to tell a fictional story (or parable) and encourage His listeners to think about deeper truths. He even occasionally explained it to His disciples!

The **fictional story** that we write about the Questor family has a basis in fact from our observation over many years of leading and preaching and of general Church experience. But when you read this, please don't be offended! This isn't a real family and none of the churches described here have ever existed. We have never visited them and you will never find them. However, you may recognise some of their characteristics and we hope you may laugh and sigh and feel challenged but look forward with hope. So please do use this book as a discussion document to help you think through any relevant issues and find ways to grow your church.

Would you dare to read this book? It's challenging; painful even. You may find in various places that we touch a **raw nerve** but maybe facing difficult truths is the starting point to a fruitful future. So, go on, dip in –we dare you!

Let's see what the Questor family finds as they begin their **exploration of church**...

TURNING THE TIDE

PHILIP BARBER AND BRIAN BARBER

Chapter One
Worship Matters

"Are we in agreement then?" Tanya asked.

He agreed reluctantly. "If you say so. I don't want any more arguments."

"It's taken you long enough," she huffed.

It was late evening. Ollie had been bathed and bedded and there had been no sound from him for over an hour. They were both relaxing over a glass of wine. It would've been a good evening if Tanya hadn't raised the matter again. Then they had covered the same old ground – her reasons; Alfie's objections. It was all really about her concern to bring Ollie up properly. Before she was pregnant, she had worked as a Care Assistant for a local charity, helping vulnerable young people with their many problems. She knew what a tough world it was to grow up in and she didn't want her baby son to be dragged down. Even though he was only six months old, she was planning a wonderful future for him where he would be a bright, personable, moral and successful human being. It was that moral bit that bothered her – how could she help him to escape the traps he'd have to face? So, despite her husband Alfie's practical, but rather prejudiced, objections, she thought the local church might help. Neither of them had been church goers, and only knew what the inside of a church building was like from attending the occasional wedding and watching TV. But maybe – just maybe – if they went on a Sunday morning, some of the Jesus stuff might rub off on their growing boy. It was worth a try.

"We'll go on Sunday then? To that church around the corner?" Tanya asked carefully.

"OK, OK. I've given in," he replied. "We'll try it. I don't know what to expect, but they should give a family a good welcome. Now let's watch some telly."

And that's how the matter was decided.

The following Sunday, Mr and Mrs Questor walked over with their young son to the large grey building whose spire imposed itself on its surroundings and whose closed doors they had passed many times on their way to the supermarket. They weren't wearing what used to be called "Sunday best," but Alfie wore his newest jeans and T-shirt and Tanya wore her most sober and sensible dress. Ollie was dressed in his finest baby suit, fed and changed, and sleeping soundly in his buggy.

Alfie helped Tanya as she struggled to carry the buggy up the steps to the large oak doors (now wide open). Two or three people followed behind and they were met by an elderly lady, smartly dressed. She said hello and shook their hands. "So far, so good," thought Tanya. But as they entered the inner door Alfie had an unfortunate encounter with a stiff-backed, immaculately-suited elderly gentleman standing in the aisle. The old boy's eyes roved disapprovingly over Alfie's T-shirt and jeans and then he turned wordlessly away. She glimpsed a spark of indignation in Alfie's eyes, but he loyally made no comment as they walked down a side aisle.

There must have been sixty or seventy people there and most of the back pews were filled. They didn't want to sit near the front – too conspicuous. People were already turning and staring and making them feel uncomfortable. Most of them were elderly and they couldn't see any other young families – so, after several minutes of embarrassing confusion, they slipped into a side pew as near to the back as possible. Tanya took Ollie out of his buggy, which she had to leave prominently in the aisle, because she didn't know what else to do with it, and held him, still asleep, as they sat down together. The people in the pew in front nodded good morning, but nothing else was said.

A guy wearing a long black robe and a Vicar of Dibley collar emerged from a door to the right of a large central table with a cross on it, which stood at the front under a rather dusty stained-glass window. They'd seen similar scenes before but had not taken them in. The table had a rail around it – 'to keep people away?' Tanya wondered.

Then six women and a man, robed in blue, filed into a pew near the front, at right angles to their own. They remained standing, and as the guy who Alfie knew was the clergyman said, "Let us worship; Hymn number 437," other people around them got to their feet, an organ somewhere at the front began to wheeze and wail, and the event started. .

In front of each of them were three books – they had black, red and grey colours, and were slotted into a sort of shelf attached to the pew in front. Alfie and Tanya had also each sat down on a further couple of sheets covered with even more printed words.

Tanya opened each of the three books in turn. They had numbered pieces of poetry in them, but by the time she'd worked out which one to use, everyone else was singing the third verse, which was surprising because the pace was slow, and the tune was dull and rather boring to her ears.

Alfie hated the sound of organs – it was so nineteenth century and it didn't relate in any way to the music he listened to. He had, of course, heard hymns before at weddings and funerals, but he didn't know the tune and he couldn't make any sense of the words; they were full of "thee" and "thou" and contained language he'd never heard used in everyday speech. So, he stood silent, really uncomfortable because he was conscious, or so he thought, that others knew he wasn't singing. Tanya did her best to sing, but the tune was so complicated – some syllables occupied two, or even three, notes, so she was very relieved when the singing came to an end. Then all the people sat down suddenly and without warning, leaving the Questors standing and on show. For the rest of the time, they struggled with this issue of when to stand up or sit down – no one made it clear.

The next thing that happened was that the clergyman started reading from a book, and the people responded with words from one of the sheets, from a place thatneither Tanya nor a rather reluctant Alfie could find. They scrambled around fretfully, scouring the sheets and turning pages of the books listlessly, while prayers, readings and statements were pronounced from the front or around them, most of which they didn't understand. "Shall we leave?" asked Alfie, but she didn't want to make a fuss and was determined to see it through.

That was about all that happened in the first half hour – standing, sitting, listening, reading, with the two Questors doing their best to keep up. They knew that they were surrounded by religious language and that it focussed on God and Jesus, but they found it difficult to understand. They didn't know what, if anything, they believed and there was nothing in that long and boring set of repetitions that spoke to them, until they came to the sermon – oh, the sermon! Tanya sat up – she had heard about sermons from religious sitcoms on telly.

The clergyman had a thin, reedy voice and delivered his words in a sing-song fashion. In their opinion it was a sort of "holy" way he had of speaking – it didn't sound like he was in touch with their everyday lives. The sermon was on something called an "epiphany" ' and he described how, on one occasion, Jesus had turned white and surprised his disciples. His theme was that when Jesus comes to us, we might be surprised, but we must do something about it. "What must be done?" thought Tanya, but there was no answer from the front. Alfie just closed his eyes and thought of footy. "It'll soon be over now," he mused, glancing at his mobile. There was a ramshackle screen to the side of the clergyman and he tried to illustrate his talk with PowerPoint projection, but the projector broke down twice and then he got confused as to where he was in his talk, so he was constantly flipping back and forth, trying to find his place. This chaos woke Alfie up (at least there was something to laugh at). Butwhen he snorted, some people turned round and glared at him, so he did his best to internalise his chuckles. "Red face; black frock," he chuckled to himself, as he stared at the poor, struggling clergyman, "rather like some crazy superhero character." The commotion had unfortunately awakened Ollie (who, deciding he was hungry, had begun to cry), and this elicited a chorus of tuts and shushes from the people behind, further embarrassing and infuriating Alfie.

After a final stand-up sit-down hymn, the show was over and they made their escape as quickly as they could. "I told you it was a waste of time," he whispered as the buggy clattered down the steps.

"We'll try somewhere else next week," she replied defiantly.

The problem is...

The quality of worship matters – it really does. When it's lacking, it can be very difficult for unchurched people to access.

It's unlikely this collection of issues would be found in one church service, but we've observed each of them in various churches over the years. Maybe you have too. Maybe you can observe some of them in your services. Try to look at your church through the eyes of someone who has rarely been to church before and who would find the whole experience difficult to access.

Tanya and Alfie found it difficult to understand what was going on for a variety of reasons:

This church seems to be geared primarily for those in the know; the regular attendees, but not to the first-time visitors. **Were they expecting or even wanting visitors?** The leader and the congregation were seeing things from their perspective and making incorrect assumptions about what visitors would like or understand. Maybe it didn't even occur to them that what they were doing would be problematic. When you are closely involved in church, it's very difficult to see things from the outside looking in(it's typical of churches that have lost their vision for making new disciples of Jesus Christ). The congregation was mainly elderly. They may possibly not have had a mission focus for a long time. Perhaps there had been a clear failure of leadership here over many years. Maybe leaders had tried but been defeated by people who had stubbornly resisted change; perhaps because they did not see the need.

Although there was a welcoming presence at the door (sadly not always the case), no one was available to show the newcomers to their seats, so they immediately felt a little awkward and embarrassed. This "first time" awkwardness is the reason why many sports clubs, restaurants and hotels will have dedicated staff to show people around and help them feel welcome. This general sense of unease was exacerbated by the old gentleman who silently expressed his disapproval of Alfie's casual dress.

Church used to be a formal occasion and "Sunday best" was the expected form of dress. This expectation creates a strong divide from modern culture which prefers "weekend casual" (increasingly "work casual" these days). Many churches have now adjusted and informal dress is much more common. To be honest there's little indication in the Bible that God has any interest in how we're dressed (Adam and Eve were naked!); being much more concerned with the state of our hearts. **Dressing**

up in the past may have been a mark of respect for being in the presence of God. Do you think that this should change in the light of modern culture?

The (unintentional) impression was given that the worship event was out of touch with modern life and the real world. There was impenetrable liturgy and archaic language which conveyed little real meaning to our twenty-first century family. There was nothing practical in the sermon to help them apply Biblical truths to their real-life journey. The sermon was also boring and poorly presented. The breakdown of the audio-visual presentation was embarrassing. The formal robes worn by the minister added to this general impression. Though clerical attire can be a helpful form of identification in certain situations (such as hospital visiting) it can also be off-putting to unchurched people. Though the "trendy vicar" label can be sneeringly applied, we think ministers should not be discouraged if their motive is to try to connect with unchurched people**. What do you think?**

The music was not of a style with which they were familiar and, to be frank, there are very few people these days who listen to organ music. The songs were in old English and used theological words no longer in common parlance – it is genuinely difficult for some people to understand what they mean ("Here I raise my Ebenezer…!").

There was a general lack of guidance about how to navigate a way through the liturgy, about which book to use and when to stand or sit. Your authors, despite a lifetime spent in church, have both experienced the embarrassing struggle of trying to find the correct page in a service book because no clear guidance was offered by the worship leader. Imagine how such embarrassment is magnified for the first time-in-church visitor.

The leader didn't welcome visitors from the front. A simple smile and acknowledgement (joke even!) would have gone a long way to making our family feel relaxed and at ease.

There were no facilities for parents with children, no place for a pushchair to be conveniently sited, no crèche during the sermon and pews which were difficult for mothers with small children to use.

The way ahead...

Is this church too far gone?

We would contend that it most certainly isn't. It has a good and viable congregation of sixty to seventy and with careful work could be moved from maintenance to mission. Very many traditional and ageing churches need not face inevitable closure if a series of simple changes and improvements are made (especially to the worship which is generally the "shop window" of church life). We would go so far as to say that, unless a church building is sited in an inappropriate place where the community it used to serve has long since disappeared, it need not close. Indeed, it mustn't. Too many churches have closed and too much ground has been lost already.

We would advise that the strategy would involve a determined but gradual programme of change. This should be accompanied by careful teaching about the primary purpose of church – making disciples – and casting a vision of how that could be accomplished. Robust but loving leadership would be required to navigate the people over some inevitable crisis points. A leader would certainly need strength of character to face up to people's objections gently but firmly; even being prepared to lose a few vocal objectors. We would suggest starting a programme of change by getting on board a small group of key people – possibly some leaders or those with leadership potential who have indicated this desire for change. These could be taught and trained in new ideas and then form a core of people who would support the new vision.

We suggest attention could be given to the following points (though we are aware human resources are limited in many churches):

1. Worship and spirituality must always be good. Simplify the liturgy, have the choir sing a beautiful song; keep it short. Because Sunday worship is the "shop window" of any church, care should be taken to improve the professionalism of the experience. High quality in everything should be a mantra.

2. If you have a good and reliable organist who can cope with modern worship songs, then that's a bonus, though organ music is a minority interest these days (and many people don't like it). Good musicians are in short supply though it is possible to find hidden gems in many congregations. If the leader has an intentional, well-publicised plan to encourage the playing of different instruments, it can be surprising how many people can be persuaded to play. People can also be persuaded to start learning an instrument if there's a culture

that encourages music and experimentation. The use of modern instruments can be controversial but a small ensemble of piano/keyboard, guitar, flute etc. will greatly enhance and modernise the worship experience. Start simply and gradually develop – that's the way forward. Bring variety by choosing some modern songs and wean a congregation to some new music.

3. Make no assumptions about what a visitor would understand. Try to make every aspect of the worship relevant to the visitor and seeker. Pay attention to the style of the worship experience, trying to imagine what it would feel like to a visitor who had never been to church before. **Ask an unchurched friend to attend and write an honest critique**. This would be a brave action and might reveal painful truths but could form the basis of an action plan. We expect people to come to our world, when, in reality, we need to be incarnated in theirs, as Jesus was in ours. It's a sacrifice.

4. Train a few volunteers to offer children's work and crèche facilities even if there are usually no children present. Do this, otherwise there will probably never be children, because any families coming for the first time would almost certainly not return if there was nothing for their children (which is a kind of vicious cycle from which it can be hard to escape). There might be a former teacher in the congregation who could offer to take assemblies at the local primary school and who could then invite parents and children to a special family service. A school choir could sing carols at Christmas. If

there's the possibility of children's work, some parents coming to such events could decide to stay.

5. In some denominations there's often a different preacher each week. A guarded pulpit may be required if consistency is to be applied to the preaching and the style of worship. This means the leaders must take control of who preaches each week, because visiting clergy or lay preachers may want to organise the worship or preaching in a manner that doesn't serve the vision of the church as it tries to connect with unchurched people.

6. Worship leaders should get into the habit of giving clear instructions about when to stand and sit, and exactly which page/book the congregation should refer to, especially if there's extensive use of liturgy. Guidance, not assumption, is crucial to avoid off-putting embarrassment. The issue isn't with liturgy per se – some people really enjoy liturgical worship and find it very helpful. The issue is when visitors get lost in a confusing collection of books and feel excluded.

7. Volunteer welcomers and hosts are roles which can enable Christians to serve and grow as well as providing a very helpful experience for the visitor. Straightforward friendly conversation at the door explaining how the service will operate can remove a sense of awkwardness or embarrassment that can discourage visitors from returning. Team members need careful training in what is appropriate and inappropriate to say. A simple script can be learnt. Guiding people to seats is very beneficial. A welcome pack with basic information

about the church and its activities is inexpensive to produce and assures visitors that they're welcome. Welcomers could wear a lanyard with their name on. Knowing a name helps visitors connect and personalise the experience.

8. Train the congregation to be accepting of different people, differences and new things. There shouldn't be any tutting, shushing or dark looks! It needs to be gently and carefully explained that church isn't a private club for the initiated but an open house which welcomes all; "whosoever will may come." Making people feel awkward because they aren't dressed appropriately is surely going to discourage them from returning.

9. Improve the Audio-Visual Aid or install one. The preacher needs an assistant to operate the computer. This could be a fun job for someone which could anchor them in church. It's a good idea for churches to move the screen and projector to present song words, liturgy, sermon notes/illustrations and pictures. The equipment is cheap to buy these days. It greatly enhances the worship experience, especially for younger visitors for whom the visual is more significant than the merely audio.

10. Training for preachers on sermon style and content is always necessary. All preachers should be learners and readers – otherwise their sermons will become stale and moribund. It's very helpful to keep sermons short and to include lots of ways that Biblical truths can be practically applied to real life. The preacher must believe what he/she preaches

because, when you preach, your true inner self is always exposed to the listeners.

11. Good preaching should be: down to earth, solid and relevant to everyday life; funny, short and pithy (some preachers talk for so long they could put a glass eye to sleep!). They should include stories and illustrations, memorable key points, clear voice and diction. The preacher needs to talk to the congregation not with her/his head down and reading word for word, but illustrate with pictures on screen, rather than long lists of points which some people sarcastically call "death by PowerPoint."

12. Encourage people to move forward and leave the back rows for visitors. Share the reason for this.

13. A small prayer group should start to meet to pray for the church and worship. This is probably the most important of all. Without prayer, nothing much of significance will happen in church life. There won't be any growth, problems will continue to arise and no one will find faith, without prayer.

Questions for discussion...

We invite readers to consider these important questions.

What is church for?

What is the primary purpose, goal, mission and vision of your church?

Is church worship for believers only?

Why have many churches in this country become populated mainly by the elderly?

Why are so many churches closing?

Can dying churches be changed or are they simply doomed to close?

And the big questions: How does a leader help a congregation to change? How can a congregation help to implement change?

Discuss any of the suggestions in the previous section which are relevant to your situation.

Make a plan to gradually introduce changes, starting with the least contentious.

In this and subsequent chapters we've highlighted additional questions buried in the text which you might find helpful to consider.

Chapter Two

Accommodation Matters

Alfie was sprawled on the settee, glued to a recording of the original "Top Gear" on the telly, when she came in from the kitchen.

"I know it's your day off," she began, "but Natalie rang and we're meeting for coffee at Costa. I'll only be there for a couple of hours."

"Natalie?" he grunted.

"Yes, from down the street. Will you keep your eye on Ollie while I'm gone?"

"Yes, yes. Whatever," he replied.

"He's asleep. You'll hear on that thing, if he disturbs. Just do the usual if he wakes; then play with him a bit before you put him down again. I'll be back soon."

She slipped her coat on and closed the front door behind her with a relieved sigh. She hadn't been completely truthful. Yes, they would go to Costa at some point, but she'd taken Nat into her confidence and they were going to inspect one of the town churches to see if it was more suitable than their last failed attempt. The two giggled over their guilty secret when they met. Tanya knew Alfie would be dismissive if she told him, but she'd decided she would work on him if she was successful. And, in any case, she'd persuaded Natalie to bring her two children with them if they found a good place.

There was a big old church at the end of the street. She knew each of these churches was a particular brand of Christianity, but she wasn't really bothered which one this was, as she didn't know what each brand meant or whether any one brand was in any way different from any other. This one was a very large rectangular building with a sloping roof and it had no spire. Its two large, dark oak doors were firmly shut and rather forbidding in appearance. Pinned to one side of the doors was a huge cardboard thermometer and a notice above read "roof fund, target £60,000." A garden wilderness ran around the front and sides – just overgrown grass and weeds – with a high, rusting railing running around it. Its front gate was padlocked, and, at first sight, there was no way in.

"Perhaps it's closed down," said Natalie cautiously.

"No," Tanya replied, "I saw some old people going in last Sunday. Both the gates and the doors were open then."

She pointed to the notice board, framed with peeling black paint. The dates of eight Sundays including the next were listed, and each had the name of a person by it. None of these names were known by either of the two women and they wondered why they were there. The only other notice on the board read, "Better is the poor that walketh in his integrity than he that is perverse in his ways, though he be rich" (Proverbs 28:6). They both read this through several times but couldn't make any sense of it.

Attached to the bottom of the board was a card; blown backwards and forwards by the wind. They could only just make out the words, "Enter by the side door." So, they walked down by the side of the railings until they came to a small, unlocked gate. Then they had to double back on themselves to find a single brown door, firmly closed. On it was a large notice which read, "Rough sleepers: This is church property. You are not allowed to sleep here. If you leave your possessions here, we will dispose of them."

"They mustn't lock the side gate," Natalie commented. "Not exactly a friendly welcome for rough sleepers."

"Alfie would hate that – he'd want to help them, not threaten them," Tanya replied. "This place is like Fort Knox. Shall we try it, though?"

Natalie nodded timorously, so Tanya tried the handle, and gave the door a firm push. It opened on to a long dark corridor, carpeted with faded lino, worn and patchy. There was a door at the far end; they looked at one another with uncertainty. Then Tanya took her courage in both hands and stepped in. She could just hear chatter and laughter beyond the far door, so she walked forward boldly, with Nat treading delicately behind her. The door opened onto a large hall, with a small proscenium stage, whose closed curtains were sagging slightly. There was a small table with a cross on it, just in front of the stage and about thirty or forty upright, metal-framed chairs facing it. At the other end was a circle of high-backed chairs very reminiscent of the kind found in old people's homes. Along one wall was a collection of mismatched cupboards and shelves piled high with an assortment of old books, papers and plastic toys. The hall was painted chocolate brown to waist height, and then a dirty cream above it. Damp was showing through in two or three places, and the floorboards were bare and dusty. There was an unpleasant damp and musty smell.

Fifteen or sixteen elderly ladies were standing around chatting, teacups in their hands. To Tanya's left was a hatch opening onto a Formica-covered counter, with a semi-large kitchen beyond it. Two women were standing behind the counter, serving tea from a large metal pot. "The place that time forgot," whispered Natalie, as all the women turned and stared at them in silence. Then a portly, smartly-dressed, grey-haired woman bustled up to them. "Welcome to the Women's Bright Hour," she said briskly. "We never have visitors, but you're very welcome. Would you like a cup of tea?"

"Er - yes," Tanya stuttered, "but could I use the facilities first?" They had both previously agreed that the state of the toilets would be a deciding factor in any building they visited.

"I'm very sorry but the toilets are out of order so the only facilities we have are outside at the end of the yard," the elderly lady replied. "I'll show you." She led them over to a far door. Both Tanya and Natalie followed meekly. The door opened on to an overgrown yard, at the bottom of which was a rather derelict shed.

"It's a chemical toilet. We try not to use it," the woman confided, "but I'll leave you to it. The meeting starts in fifteen minutes," and she turned and left them alone. They looked at one another in horror; then they grinned. "I think I'll wait," said Natalie laughing. "I bet the spiders in there are huge! What do you think of the setup?"

"Well, the women seem pleasant enough, but the building..."

"We've got to go back that way. The back yard is shut off – there are padlocked gates on both sides. There's no other way out."

"Let's have a cup of tea and a chat and then excuse ourselves," Tanya said. "I can't see Alfie liking this place."

So, they joined the queue for tea – just four women in front of them. When they reached the hatch, Tanya noticed one or two greasy surfaces in the kitchen, with dirt ingrained into the corners. It didn't look as though they had a caretaker, and the Bright Hour just seemed to make do. She thought it surprising. "I bet they keep their homes better than this," she thought. "If I drink anything, will I be ill?"

The two of them stood by the hatch sipping stewed tea. One or two of the other women gave them furtive looks, but no one came across to converse.

"Well, ladies, we'll begin," said the woman who had first greeted them loudly, and, as the Bright Hour took their seats, Tanya and Natalie made their escape.

The door by which they had first entered had a tatty piece of paper pinned to the inside. Scrawled in longhand on it were the words, "Turn the toilet light off!"

"Very polite," said Natalie sarcastically. "The people seem nice enough, but not very friendly. And the building... who wants to use premises like that in the twenty-first century?"

The problem is...

This is an amalgamation of accommodation horrors, but all these can affect the visitor to church**. Who wants to use or even enter poorly maintained premises?** Only the faithful few will put up with, or maybe not even notice, decrepit facilities. Your authors have seen premises where many of these horrors described have been evident. Sadly, somewhere they could all be seen. **How about you?**

We would suggest that it's very difficult indeed to attract people to church if the accommodation is poor. These days when we go to restaurants or hotels, we expect a certain level of comfort and cleanliness or we don't return. Trip advisor has brought increasing pressure and expectation on companies to provide good facilities, and churches are competing in the marketplace whether we like it or not. A famous comedian once joked, "Garden centres are the places people go to now on Sundays instead of church!" This is the reality we face.

The whole accommodation described in the story would have given an impression of old fashioned "make do and mend," dirtiness and general neglect. "Is it still open?" would no doubt have been a question in the minds of passers-by. Such neglect as this in real life churches attracts vandalism and discourages most people from attending even if they are genuinely searching for God. Regular church attenders can become oblivious to the poor accommodation. This may be because they lack financial or human resources or maybe because they have become so used to the place that they no longer notice its faults and they long ago stopped looking at it with the eyes of a visitor. Of course, some church members are well aware of the shortcomings of their building but are elderly or have become weary trying to maintain large and often old premises. We have great sympathy with the faithful few struggling on, but it can be a vicious cycle – poor quality accommodation means a visitor won't return, so the congregation gradually declines and there's even less money for, and help with, improvements. Outreach then becomes pointless if the accommodation is poor, because people won't come and any effort is wasted. We suggest that it's best to bring church premises, or at least part of them, up to an acceptable standard before other projects are considered.

There's a strange culture in some churches where people buy a nice new thing for their house and offer the tatty old thing it replaced to the church. **Who wants tatty old rubbish? Why not buy something new for God and make do with the old for yourself?** In the book of Haggai God strongly criticises the Jews for this very thing:

'Is it a time for you yourselves to be living in your panelled houses, while this house remains in ruin?' *Haggai 1:4*

Christians must rise to this challenge if they are to have much hope of saving their church from closure.

Toilets need a special mention because they are of crucial importance and are sometimes in a really awful state. The toilets in our story were completely unacceptable, and people, especially women, won't return if the toilets are foul. If money can be found, toilet refurb is top priority (as long as the building is structurally sound), so that they are clean, fresh and pleasant with feminine hygiene, baby changing and disabled access made available.

In our story, we tried to suggest that there was a certain amount of fear experienced by the elderly and faithful congregation – hence the harsh notice to rough sleepers. This is understandable and a congregation facing such difficult issues should access support from outside agencies rather than posting angry notices. Angry notices run the risk of provoking an unpleasant response in others and send the wrong message to visitors.

It is easy to spot many dreadful examples of notice boards outside churches all around the country. Almost nothing else gives a worse impression of neglect than faded, out of date, old fashioned, stuck on with Sellotape, torn notices on shabby boards. It's better to have none if they can't be maintained properly.

The name of an event is really important, and a name like "Women's Bright Hour" for example, sounds too much like past times of those brought up in the 1960s and beyond. They go to rock concerts, drink coffee in quality trendy establishments, surf the web and take international holidays. There are still some leaders who imagine that such people will return to traditional churches when they reach their retirement years – they are greatly deluded. Very few of these people will. Older people will then have to be won over, just like younger people. Careful thought needs to be given to the name of every activity in church to ensure that it's attractive and enticing to the non-churchgoer.

The way ahead...

Some denominations have large funds to help with refurbishment projects, but some do not, and small, elderly congregations can be left struggling to fund essential repairs. However, small changes which don't cost a lot can make a huge difference.

For worn-out premises, we would suggest the leaders formulate a five to ten year plan which is proactive not reactive – linked to a mission strategy, and asking first the question: **What is God's will for this church?**

We suggest attention is given to the following:

1. Review the notice boards and make them attractive. Refresh regularly – no out of date notices. There should be no old-fashioned quotes, particularly those that are negative and threaten hell to the unbeliever. It's sufficient to be simple. For example, post the name of the church and a welcome or add a simple strap line: there are plenty of excellent examples online. Names of preachers are meaningless to the outsider, so don't show them.

2. Remove the money begging thermometer and all references to that inside. "The church is only after our money!" is a rather harsh but often expressed opinion by non-church goers, and a thermometer only reinforces this untruth.

3. Remove junk and rubbish from the area surrounding the church/car park. Kill all the weeds and remove the stubble. Any unkempt appearance is easily and cheaply changed. **Could a working party be organised by a neighbouring church or**

local school if this work is beyond an elderly congregation? Ask for help; there is a lot of good will around. A further development of this idea is to invite the local community to create a community garden. This can be a great way to make friends and improve the look of the church yard.

4. The accommodation is described by our two visitors as the place that time forgot. Invite an outsider to describe what is wrong with what they see, and then try to decorate and modernise one key meeting space. A concealed entrance excludes or discourages visitors, so make sure it's easily accessible. Alternatively, make the main worship area multi-use – clean, freshly painted and clear of rubbish (Again, **ask your friendly independent visitor to identify what they see as rubbish** – it might be something you thought was part of the much-loved church furniture!). This may involve the removal of pews, for example, and in some denominations, permission should be sought.

5. If money is available, replace the grim oak doors with reinforced glass doors to give the appearance that the place isn't closed and to let in light.

6. Internal notices should be replaced (if possible) by a screen linked to a scrolling PowerPoint presentation showing the activities of the church, which is sited in the foyer. Remove notices on scraps of paper plastered over walls and doors.

7. Toilets, especially women's toilets, are absolute priority – it's where any money should be spent next, after essential repairs to the roof, etc.

8. Think carefully about the name of every event in church life**. Does it need updating?** Form a small team to brainstorm new names. There are plenty of good examples on the web. **Ask your unchurched friend to comment on any name you choose before it's used.**

9. Some buildings are so far gone they need a complete update – electrics, plumbing, heating etc. **Could a small church move into a home or rent a community centre if no large grants are available? Could the church be shared by community groups who help with refurbishment or could a new congregation share the space?**

10. Remove mouldy old hymn books, papers and shelves piled with stuff. Any meeting room should be clean and freshly painted and with appropriate floor covering. As far as possible, remove storage cupboards from the main room and store things out of sight. Chairs set out like an old folks' home give the wrong impression and if possible, should be stored out of sight when not in use.

11. Kitchen cleanliness is a big issue and hygiene, health and safety should always be addressed.

12. There are many other issues with older buildings such as: disabled access, fire safety, health concerns (Legionella and asbestos), Portable Appliance Testing, damp and so on. The cost of putting these things right may well be prohibitive for a small and elderly congregation and difficult decisions sometimes must be made about the viability of buildings. Money remains an issue,

whatever the size or age of the congregation, and it's of course only possible to work within the budget, though some of the changes described above can be tackled through church or community volunteers. The leader/pastor/vicar/priest/minister will need a strategic plan, which may involve grant funding, volunteer help and district, diocesan, regional or national financial or practical help. It's quite a challenge and could require a medium or long-term plan, but some of this could be tackled short term, while the longer term is still pending.

13. At the time of writing there are emerging stories of traditional churches mainly in villages which are opening their space for community use. This involves removing pews and putting in moveable chairs to create space in the week for groups to use. This is particularly relevant where other community facilities such as village post offices, shops and halls are closing. Some churches are putting in a prayer space at one end of the church during the week with candles to light etc. There is evidence that as people are using the prayer space they are beginning to engage with faith and some even beginning to turn up on Sunday for worship, leading to a gradual renewal of the church community. **Could your church explore this idea?**

Questions for discussion...

We invite readers to take a careful look around their church premises.

What simple improvements could be made to make your place more welcoming and accessible to visitors?

What is God's plan for your church premises? Ask Him.

How could kerb appeal (the attractiveness of a property and its surrounding when viewed from the street) be improved?

Ask an unchurched friend to comment on the accommodation and critique it.

Formulate a five to ten year plan to improve your building as funds allow; starting with what you consider to be the most pressing needs.

Chapter Three
Communication Matters

Alfie knew his wife really well. She was a single-minded and determined woman who loved her little family. He guessed she was still pursuing this church idea. He thought he'd surprise her by investigating himself. There was a modern-ish looking church about a mile from his place of work; right in the centre of town. The building looked as though it was put up in the sixties. It had plain glass front doors, so he peered in one day when he was wandering around during his lunch hour. You could see right down the central aisle to a large, illuminated cross on the far wall. There were modern, comfortable, padded chairs in rows, facing this cross. Its notice board, on the outside wall to the left of the doors, advertised a half-hour service every Wednesday at 12:45 pm, "for workers." There was a car park, barrier down, with a notice board that had red words on a black background: "For the use of church members only." He told himself that he could understand that, in a town where free parking was a premium; but he didn't need it. If he did a quick sprint from his factory, he would easily make it.

The nearer it got to Wednesday, the more nervous and unsure he became. It was a big step to cross that threshold alone; not knowing what exactly to expect or whom he'd meet. It wouldn't be like the camaraderie of his biker mates or the local pub (of that he was sure), but he told himself he'd survived one disaster and it surely couldn't be any worse, could it? In any case, he wanted to surprise and please Tanya and he had his own secret reasons for going.

Wednesday arrived. It was a grey, grizzly day. He didn't have a coat, so he dodged in and out of shop doorways, wishing he could get something to eat from Subway as he passed, but there was no time. As it was, he was a few minutes late, arriving rather damp and dishevelled. He peered in. There were twenty or so people sitting, heads bowed, on the first two rows of seats and a clergyman in a grey robe standing at the front; half-turned towards the cross. He slipped in – the place was totally silent. As he lowered himself into the nearest chair, the clergyman said a loud "Amen." The people raised their heads and several half-turned to stare at him. No one smiled, and he felt rather uncomfortable and conspicuous. One man got up and walked towards him, a little stiffly. He must have been in his seventies, grey haired and bespectacled. "We don't sit at the back on a Wednesday," he said, rather too loudly. "Come forward. We'll wait." The congregation continued to stare and the clergyman was silent. Red-faced and reluctant, Alfie got up and moved what seemed a very long way to a chair immediately behind the congregation.

"Right!" said the clergyman, "We'll continue." He sounded slightly irritated. "We will sing Hymn 432, 'Day By Day We Magnify Thee.'" The organ struck up and the service continued. The parts Alfie could understand seemed to focus on finding God in the workplace – how, he didn't know. It was clear that the people in front of him were largely elderly and probably retired. Why they wanted to find God in the workplace was puzzling. They all looked as though they knew what they were doing; as though they were completely familiar with the procedure. However, no one turned to help him as he struggled to find his way through the various hymn books and prayer books referred to. That didn't bother him as much as the growing feeling that he was an alien in a foreign land and intruding into a private club; not really wanted nor accepted. This was underlined by the church notices, delivered without enthusiasm from the front by the clergyman, until he announced the time of the Sunday services, including something called "the Eucharist." He became considerably more energised, as he asked people to give generously on the plate that was passed around. The plate was pushed under Alfie's nose and he fumbled in his pocket for a 50p piece which he dropped self-consciously onto it. The rest of the notices were about various weekly activities: a Bible study, Zumba and Pilates, a musical concert and so on. The only notice that interested Alfie was that a cup of tea was provided at the back of the church when the service was over. The clergyman attempted to make light of these notices by cracking a few jokes that passed over Alfie's head (mostly about a woman called "Betty," who seemed to be at the centre of every activity). In fact, most of what happened passed Alfie by; it didn't address the problems he had at work and he couldn't see how this God they were supposed to be worshipping could possibly be interested in him.

But this time he had a different aim – he wanted to get to know people. So, when the proceedings had finished, he approached a group chatting in the aisle. "Hi!" he said, rather nervously. They turned and looked at him, greeted him and then turned back to continue their conversation. Alfie stood there for a while with his hands in his pockets and then he wandered off to get a cup of tea. The woman who was serving said, "Sugar's on the table over there, dear" and then turned to serve someone else. Alfie felt alone. It all seemed so unfriendly. He stirred sugar into his tea rather disconsolately and then, to his surprise, was addressed by an elderly woman standing at his elbow. The conversation went like this:

"Good afternoon! Is this your first time?"

"Yes, it is."

"Did you enjoy it?"

"Well... er... it was different."

"I'm Betty. Everyone knows me. Would you like to buy a ticket for the concert next week?"

"Er... I'll have to ask my wife first."

"Let me know if she's interested."

That was the end of the conversation and Betty drifted away.

Alfie felt depressed. Although he hadn't told Tanya, he was inwardly glad when she started searching for a church for Ollie's sake. He came from a dysfunctional family and Tanya had lost both parents and had no siblings. He was searching for warmth, friendship and family. He hadn't found it in the loose relationships with bikers, pub mates and work colleagues. If it was going to be anywhere, it would be in a church. After all, these people really believed in love. He expected them to make the first move; at least to express interest in him as a human being and he'd hoped their approach would help him overcome his natural shyness. He really wanted to be part of things. However, this place was like a club – they related to one another, but wouldn't let him in. He felt that he was trying hard, but surely it was their job to open themselves up to him. Wasn't that what church was all about?

He shrugged his shoulders, opened a glass door and stepped out into the real world. He was going to be late back at work, to no avail. The glass doors spoke back at him, "Look – but don't touch!"

The problem is...

In this chapter we raise a question which is quite controversial: **Is church primarily for the benefit of those not yet in it?** Some would argue that church is first and foremost the place for believers to worship the living God and that it's through this activity that new disciples are made. This is a fair point. However, while worship is of course a vital activity for believers, we maintain that the primary thrust of church life should be towards those who aren't yet part of it. Indeed, as American writer Thom S. Rainer had said: "When the preferences of the church members are greater than their passion for the Gospel, the church is dying." Whilst we would acknowledge this to be true, we also acknowledge how desperately difficult it can be to persuade some church members of this truth. Jesus' Great Commission to His followers is very clear:

"Therefore, go and make disciples of all nations; baptising them in the name of the Father and of the Son and of the Holy Spirit and teaching them to obey everything I have commanded you." – Matthew 28:19-20

As Christians, we know this well enough, but it's difficult to follow this principle in practice; especially if there's been little outward focus in a church for many years. **Where do you think the people in your church stand in this regard?**

Jesus clearly didn't intend for the church to be a self-serving community. Most Christians know this, which is why churches all over the world are engaged in so much mission work. This can be expressed both in terms of direct evangelism and in good works. Clothing the naked, feeding the hungry, visiting prisoners and being Good Samaritans all occupy a huge proportion of the life of most church communities. All this work is mostly for the benefit of people who aren't church members at all. **So, if this is already the reality of church life, why not just admit it and style our worship services with unchurched people in mind?** Here is the rub though: Many Christians like their worship services, enjoy them and get great benefit from them. We wonder what God thinks about this. **Is worship for Christians or for God? Would God prefer our focus to be on trying to win unchurched people to faith?**

In our story Alfie went to a service advertised as being "for workers," yet it was clearly styled for the believer and therefore was of no help to him. Indeed, it probably did more harm than good. Communicating with seekers and helping them towards faith is a difficult art to master. **If a service is billed as being for those in work, would a short presentation followed by discussion type activities be better than just a regular service? Rather**

than a formal seating arrangement, would a coffee bar style be more appropriate?

In order to deal with visitors successfully, it's necessary to give the matter careful consideration, and then to train church members in how to handle themselves. Alfie was rudely rejected by people who were only interested in their own friendships. Cliques form very easily in church, whether traditional or contemporary, but there's a responsibility on all Christians, clergy and people alike, to be open and welcoming to newcomers. After all, it's not the responsibility of the newcomer to make friends; that responsibility lies with those who need to show the love of God to all (In this story, you'd have noted that the clergyman didn't make any effort to speak to the only newcomer.). **Was that tight little group of churchgoers embarrassed because they didn't know what to say?** We can't believe that people who have families and jobs couldn't put together a few friendly questions and statements and draw him into their circle. No, it was more likely to have been selfishness or thoughtlessness. Sadly, this happens in churches far too often. Alfie had a genuine need that wasn't discerned by anyone in the church – he was genuinely looking for friendship (even if, on the surface, it didn't appear to be the case). It's so easy to make false assumptions about people based on how they look or because they seem out of place and nervous. A lot of people have hidden needs and come to church to find answers and there are huge opportunities to lead them to faith. Betty's only interest in him appeared to be to get something from him. In reality, she was probably a very kind lady who needed some training in how to approach visitors. We believe that friendliness and finding friends is one of the most significant contributory factors in church growth. Sadly, what was communicated during this service was that the church was an unfriendly place, which was the precise opposite of the intention. **How friendly is your church to outsiders? Are visitors left standing alone and feeling awkward during coffee time? Are there friendship cliques? Is greeting work conducted by a small minority of Christians and blithely ignored by the majority? Ask a friend who isn't known in your church to turn up one Sunday and test it out.**

The lack of training was also apparent in the comment, "Sugar's on the table." **Where was the servant heart in this church? Why not bring the sugar to him?** It becomes evident that there's a failure on the part of the leadership to prepare the church members to care for visitors. Simple hospitality done well, can make a huge difference to the feeling of love and friendliness in a church. It's not rocket science.

The old gentleman who offered well-meant but incompetent instructions to "come forward" didn't realise how insensitive he was. Many visitors like to be anonymous and drawing attention to them is likely to be so embarrassing that they simply won't return. This illustrates the point that good intentions aren't enough; there must always be good practice. It's probably true to say that many Christians unintentionally put people off through thoughtless, but well-meaning behaviour.

There's a truth which can be hard to swallow: The church isn't a private club. If Christians want private clubs, they should play golf or Bridge or something. Church isn't the place for that. Notices which invite people to "go to Betty" for tickets, create the feeling that there's an "in crowd" who know the secrets of the private club. Visitors are excluded because they have no idea who "Betty" is. Inside jokes further emphasise the private club impression and make visitors feel excluded. Great care should always be taken to include people; especially during church notices.

The clergyman showed some irritation with Alfie because he didn't know what to do and had disturbed the proceedings. This is another mistake. Newcomers very easily pick up such subliminal signals and can be offended. A service, especially one ostensibly for visitors, should be full of smiling, greeting and patience. Tolerance of inappropriate or challenging behaviour has its limits, of course and there should be team members trained to deal firmly but gently with this.

Whether to have an offering or not is another contentious issue. In the context of an outreach service, a retiring offering would definitely be more appropriate, **but what about on a normal Sunday?** Your authors have attended a church where there wasn't any plate passed round for over twenty-five years, because the leaders felt it was inappropriate to ask visitors to contribute to the life of a church that should be fully supported by the committed believers. Perhaps giving by direct debit is a better way, with a retiring offering for those who still prefer cash. When visitors realise they're not being forced to donate, but can give if they wish, what is gained is an atmosphere free of embarrassment for them and which contradicts the lie that "they're only after our money." It seems that we're gradually moving into a cashless society; people don't always carry cash anymore. This provides additional challenges to churches and charities to provide the opportunity to pay via electronic means.

The way ahead...

The focus of our advice here is on styling a meeting specifically for the visitor; though much of the guidance could also be applied to a Sunday service.

1. 1. It might be wise to avoid spoken church notices which refer to in-house events if the meeting is supposed to be for visitors. The exception could be if there was something relevant to announce like an "Alpha" or "Only Looking" course. If there's a need to inform the regular congregation, this could be done via a printed leaflet or onscreen.

2. Instead of asking people to go to a named person, have a welcome desk at the back with information about all the church activities and sign-up sheets. This could be staffed before and after the meeting by a smiling volunteer. The table could also stock a small selection of pamphlets about the Christian faith.

3. Have spotters in the congregation, from teenagers to older people, who are on the look-out for visitors. These are pastoral team members who have been trained to chat to people, especially in more informal moments, like during refreshment time.

4. The training for team members should include advice about how to keep a conversation going. A list of open-ended questions can be produced and learnt by team members. This helps to avoid the dreaded awkward silence when neither side can think of anything to say (see Appendix 1).

5. It's a good idea to organise a training session for church members so that they understand that they should always try to show love and a welcoming approach to visitors.

6. Refreshments are important, so make sure they're good quality. No stewed tea from a metal pot! A bean to cup coffee maker which uses ethically sourced coffee is inexpensive and easy to use. The coffee culture is very popular in our society at present and people expect a decent cup. Serve fresh fruit and pastries sometimes as a change from biscuits.

7. It's advisable to transition to modern, comprehensible language. Even though many older worshippers struggle to accept a modern translation of the Bible/prayer book, most visitors will struggle even more to comprehend the Authorised Version.

8. A café-style meeting is fairly easy to organise. Set up round tables and good refreshments served by smiling helpers. A short, thought-provoking presentation would have been the best in a "workers" service. A question-and-answer session could sometimes be helpful, as would a testimony or video clip. Questions should be open to allow people to explore issues of faith rather than feeling that they're being corralled in a certain direction.

9. Gather a small team to plan the meetings. The team should have an agreed set of goals and absolute clarity of purpose. The team should pray together.

10. Station someone who can greet people at the door with a smile.

11. If your event is targeted at a particular group of people, ask them what questions they are puzzling over and try to deal with them in the talks and discussions.

12. We invite you to think about the concept of "warmth." This is an atmosphere where visitors feel welcomed, comfortable and relaxed, whatever the style of worship. If they feel like this, they're much more likely to return. We hope that if you implement some of the suggestions above, you can create such an atmosphere.

Questions for discussion...

You might like to consider the following questions:

Has your church got a mission statement (increasingly a requirement in some denominations)?

Is the mission statement well known by the congregation and do most of them subscribe to it?

How could you create a warm and welcoming atmosphere in your church?

Do you have any activities that will truly help people to journey towards faith?

Is your church merely treading water or moving forward?

If your church does have some activities which are mainly for the benefit of those people not yet in it, why not ask those people what they think? People generally love to give their opinions and their thoughts might enable church leaders to hone activities to be even more helpful to those searching for faith.

PHILIP BARBER AND BRIAN BARBER

Chapter Four
Programme Matters

"You won't see me going there again. Those people only care about themselves. They call themselves Christians!" Alfie huffed. He'd finished his story about his mid-week nightmare. He was bruised and hurt by the experience. He'd felt himself deliberately excluded; made to think he wasn't good enough for their company. He felt rejected. His voice was loud and he kept walking up and down the kitchen in an agitated fashion. His wife was really upset to see him like this; it was the opposite of what she'd intended. She did her best to calm him down.

"I don't think all churches are like that," she said timidly.

"Huh!"

"I'm sure we can find somewhere better. Don't give up."

"I'm leaving you to it. Just tell me if you ever find anywhere worth looking at. You're on your own. I'm not going through all that again," he blustered and he sank down into his favourite armchair.

"Well," she said, "I have tried a place out of town. There was a notice in the supermarket advertising a fair to raise money for Cancer Relief and it was at a church, so I went with Natalie."

"Did they cast you into outer darkness?" he asked sardonically.

"Well, I don't think there was anyone from the church there," she replied. "It was only a small place; just a chapel really. There was one large room and a kitchen and toilets – quite modern, quite clean and nice. They had their Sunday meetings in this large hall where the fair was. They'd just pushed the chairs to the side and put up some stalls. I talked to one or two of the stallholders about the chapel, but they didn't really know anything. I don't think any of them went. It seems the chapel hired out the hall for the fair. They said it was quite cheap and lots of local organisations do the same. One woman said she thought that was how the chapel kept going. Apparently, they don't have a lot of churchgoers."

"Not much point in that then," he mumbled.

"We bought a home-made cake, and some jams and everything was given by the locals, so they made a good bit for Cancer Relief," was her riposte. "And there was a noticeboard in the hall..."

"Loads of activities then? The God botherers on the march?"

"Your sarcasm!" she replied, rolling her eyes. "No – just one scrappy piece of paper, in biro writing, but it might be of some use. It said that there's a "parent and toddlers" meeting every Tuesday morning, so I thought I'd take Ollie there next Tuesday. If there are other kids, he might enjoy it and he needs to get gradually socialised. I could chat to some of the mums. Surely at least one or two of them belong to the chapel. I could find out what's going on there."

"Rather you than me. Enjoy!" he said dismissively.

The following Tuesday, Tanya pushed Ollie in his buggy for about a mile to the little chapel. It was a warm, pleasant morning and both enjoyed the air. Ollie was in a good mood, full of smiles, content and settled. They arrived about twenty minutes early for a half past ten start. There were already half a dozen mums, one dad and some rather noisy small children gathering in the hall. There was a large mat on the floor, covered in toys. Parents were placing their children on it and then getting a cup of tea and a biscuit and sitting on the upright chairs around the edges of the mat. Tanya was thankful that the atmosphere was relaxed and quite friendly. A small, bright-eyed woman seemed to be in charge, with several middle-aged female helpers. The first woman was welcoming everyone and taking down names. She greeted Tanya in a friendly fashion and said she was glad to see her. Her name was Marion and Tanya introduced her to Ollie, who was much more interested in the other children and their toys. She placed him on the mat and he began to play with some brightly-coloured building blocks, quite content to amuse himself alone. She sat down near him and began to chat to the woman on the chair next to her, who turned out to be a single mum who lived in a terraced house in a nearby avenue. She was very chatty and Tanya didn't have to ask many questions to find out what she wanted to know. This gathering of parents and offspring wasn't run by the chapel, and, just like the Cancer Relief organisation, Marion hired the hall, and gathered subs from the parents to pay for it. She was, apparently, a very community-minded person, who had identified a need in the area and had made efforts to address it. She didn't attend the chapel and there was, in fact, only one mum who went to worship there and only infrequently. "They're mostly rather elderly on Sundays. Nothing much for families," her neighbour sniffed. "But they do try to do their bit for others. They run a lunch club for pensioners on a Thursday and they let the special needs people have the hall for free on a weekly basis. There are a couple of families with teenagers and they've done sponsored events for orphans in Romania. They're a good lot really."

"Why don't you go then?" asked Tanya.

"Too busy. They say that it's not very interesting. And I'm not really religious. But they do some good work."

Tanya moved herself to sit by the woman identified as a chapel-goer. She was a serious, rather quiet woman. She hadn't got much to say about the worship activities of the chapel. They had a young pastor, who worked there part-time while he was studying. She thought he cared and visited, but couldn't preach. She was more enthusiastic about the chapel's social activities. They didn't seem very well planned or organised, but she thought it flowed from caring hearts. But Tanya had already heard the total of their activities and, apart from these non-church mums and toddlers, there didn't seem much for Alfie or herself to get involved in. She was rather disappointed, because for the first time she had thought there might be some life and interest here for both of them. There was a Bible study and prayer meeting one evening, but she didn't feel ready for heavy religiosity yet. It seemed that the surrounding community and the chapel didn't really relate. The chapel hired out its premises (presumably to make money), but almost no one from the congregation was ever seen at any of the activities. Three or four people from the chapel ran the luncheon club. They worked really hard to give the pensioners a good meal (according to her neighbour), but the attendees, while appreciative, didn't get involved with the chapel at all. There was a sort of "iron curtain" between chapel and community and only a few found their way from one to another.

The hour passed pleasantly enough though and Tanya thought she wouldn't mind coming again. It wasn't quite what she had in mind for Ollie – she wanted him to grow up surrounded by good people. She still needed a church of all the ages with a programme of community involvement and she was curious to discover what Christians believed. Nevertheless, she was determined to report back to Alfie. This could be a little step forward. Maybe it was worth giving Sunday worship a go.

The problem is...

What we're trying to show in this chapter is that there can sometimes be a disconnect between spiritual and social life and/or between church people and their community. **How do you balance spiritual activities and social ones?** This is another potentially contentious issue. We would strongly maintain that church isn't just a free social service. Of course we should love and care for people, but if this is the only thing we do, we won't make many new disciples and eventually there will be no one left to care anyway. Surely the Gospel must be preached alongside a programme of activities which help people explore faith, make a commitment to follow Jesus and learn to become His disciples. Yet this is precisely the blind spot in the ministry of many leaders we have observed. They try so hard and are genuinely motivated by love, yet, because there is no evangelical thrust to their work, the churches they lead struggle to make any headway at all. So, churches like the one in our story may have lost their way and will probably experience a gradual demographic decline and eventual closure, unless they rebalance their programme with some attempts to reach people who lie outside the bounds of the church. **We think this is truly heart-breaking. How about you?**

We would further maintain that most social care programmes run by the church should make clear in whose name they are taking place and offer the opportunity to find faith – either directly or indirectly. The way to do this is by the existing church members attending various community events held in the church, making friends and sharing the Gospel in an acceptable way to non-church goers (assuming they are willing and able of course; though it is the work of the leader to persuade the unwilling and train them). It seems that the church in Britain has a huge approval rating among the general populace because of all the good works it does. This creates so many opportunities and many people will listen if they are chatted to in friendly fashion, because they have already been recipients of the love of Christ. We can be passing up so many openings if we fail to make full use of what is often right on our doorstep. **What opportunities for evangelism have been created by the social care programmes in your church?**

There are some advantages to hiring out the premises to community groups. It creates greater contact with the community, finances for the church and allows the Holy

Spirit to continue His work in the good things non-believers do while not always recognising Him. However, hiring out the premises just so that you can pay the bills isn't by itself sufficient to fulfil Jesus' instruction to make disciples and will not provide a future for the church. Numbers will gradually dwindle and the congregation shrinks. We see this tragedy in churches up and down the country – there are even brand-new premises where the congregation has become small as the faithful have passed away. It's time for a fundamental change in the attitude of both leaders and members in such churches. There are other disadvantages too, such as the difficulty of exercising oversight of the use of the premises, the need for a paid person or helper to organise this, balancing the needs of the community with the needs of the church and making sure all organisations who use the premises are sound and safe. These disadvantages may make hiring out more complicated than it seems on first inspection.

There is a hint in the story that there was a young and inexperienced pastor working part-time while completing his studies. **Is this ever a good idea?** Perhaps this particular pastor needed to balance his academic study with the practical aspects of how to create a programme that grew God's Kingdom. There were opportunities right in front of his nose which he could seize. Without a doubt, he should have been appearing at as many of the activities taking place on the church premises as he could; encouraging the leaders and chatting to the people and providing a link between community and Kingdom. The surrounding community and the chapel needed to relate to one another and it's an important part of a paid staff member's role to help to make the links.

Perhaps our student pastor was doing all this. Tanya is to discover more about this as her story unfolds. **If you are a church leader, do you make time to visit the community activities happening on your premises? Could you develop a pastoral team to do this?**

Being a Christian is more than attending church on a Sunday. There is a need for growth as a disciple; for Bible study, prayer, home groups, youth, mums and toddlers, family events and senior citizens events on a weekly basis. The danger is that any one of these could become inward-looking and keep non-Christians out. It doesn't have to be this way. Bible studies, for example, could form the basis for growth. **Could a Bible study be opened up into an only-looking course? Could life groups/home groups/cells become open?** The small group structure is one of the key ways to strengthen and grow any church, especially if it's welcoming of newcomers.

Youth activities like Scouts/Girl Guides and Boys/Girls Brigade are wonderful and important works which really help young people to grow up with a good moral foundation and long may they continue. But if there's no link between these activities and the church, and no church-led, evangelistic youth work to which young people can go, there's little prospect that most, if any, will become disciples of Jesus Christ. Churches might claim to have a lot of children and young people coming onto their premises, but if they don't regularly come to church on Sunday, it's unlikely that they will go on to form the congregation of the future. If we want many young people to grow into responsible adulthood (many of whom will marry, have children and create the church of the future), we have got to provide a directly spiritual programme of activities which help them to think through the Gospel and give a personal response. Youth clubs, where there are only such activities as table tennis, snooker and social events, don't deliver this result either and though such clubs can serve a useful socialising purpose, the young people attending come for the fun; not to find out about Jesus. Clubs like this don't generally deliver young disciples for the church, but there are ways to do youth work which do.

The way ahead...

The church that Tanya went to didn't seem to have tackled these issues in any strategic way. What it could offer was limited because it was small, but its leaders needed to think through how it might effectively do some of the things listed above and make them really work. We suggest the following ideas could be tried if your church faces a similar situation:

1. Offer a balanced evangelistic and social care programme. If you want to have people of all ages in your church, then you should put on activities to cater for them. So, this aspect of a church's programme also needs careful planning.

2. Make sure that you maximise opportunities to chat about Jesus in every activity the church runs.

3. Try to ensure that every activity run by the church is of good quality. Some people make negative decisions about faith based on what they see in church life.

4. Talk to the people who live around your church and find out what their real needs are. Perhaps you could even conduct a survey. Cancel meetings which are poorly attended or seem to serve no real purpose anymore, in order to make space and energy for more relevant activities. **This can be painful but if there's little or no fruit, what's the point in doing it?**

5. Explain to the congregation how important it is that they involve themselves in groups which hire their building, like parents and toddlers. Give teaching on the servant heart of Jesus to reinforce the message and gradually persuade church members to get involved.

6. Train the congregation on how to chat about Jesus in a non-threatening way. Equip them with possible ways of dealing with some of the "big questions" people might ask.

7. Create small groups. These groups form an excellent way to grow church when they're open to non-believers. People often find an informal setting the most helpful way to make friends and open up about issues which are important to them.

8. Put on a course designed to help non-believers journey towards faith. The Alpha course is one good example, but there are others.

Questions for discussion...

Here are some more questions for discussion:

Why is quality important in any programme of activities?

What opportunities are you missing to share the Gospel in your existing programme?

Examine the weekly programme in your church and consider whether you need a better balance between evangelistic and social activities.

Please see Appendix 3 for some guidance about personal evangelism.

Chapter Five

Life Matters

Alfie leaned forward in his chair and repeated with vehemence, "No, I'm not going, and that's that."

Tanya had paid a Sunday visit to the little out-of-town chapel. She'd been disappointed yet again. There were between forty and fifty people there – some older, some younger. There were a couple of young families in the congregation, but no child was as young as Ollie. It was what she could now recognise as a traditional service. The premises were modern, plain and in good repair. The young man who led the service was very good at explaining what was happening, but there was only one hymn book to refer to. There was an organ and an organist, an elderly woman, who played with gusto and who drowned out all the singers. The children were told a story that pointed to Jesus and the man gave a reasonably interesting talk just before the last hymn. She was treated to a polite "hello" when she arrived and nobody stared at her during the service. But she had this overwhelming feeling that the event was completely dead. Everyone seemed to be going through the motions, behaving as though they'd done this many times before (as they probably had) and that they weren't really interested in it. There was no life, no spark anywhere and she wondered if they really believed what they were sitting through. She even noticed a few people scrolling through their mobile phones. The young man did his best; his jokes were met with silence and she noted that, when he gave his talk, people were passing sweets to one another, as though seeking a comfortable way of getting through. She didn't close her eyes during the prayers and she noticed several others just glancing around as though they weren't listening. The whole experience was as though this God they were supposed to believe in had been frozen out of the proceedings.

But as she sat there, she had a big idea. She would invite two or three of the younger women to meet her for coffee one morning, ask them about the chapel and try to find out if they did believe anything. So, when it came to the chapel's own coffee time at the end of the service, she approached a group of women (probably around their fifties in age) and began a conversation. They were quite chatty and as it turned out, often met one another on a Tuesday morning in Costa. They invited her to join them.

However, when she told Alfie about this later, he became very agitated. She hadn't expected him to come anyway, even though he was on a late shift that day. But he made clear he wasn't going to meet with any so-called "Christians," who, from his experience, were less friendly and open than the people he met in his daily life; he didn't want to be hurt again. So, on Tuesday morning, she put Ollie in his buggy, and pushed him to Costa, where she found three other women waiting. They re-introduced themselves as Alison, Beth and Marge. They all ordered their drinks, and carried them to an empty table and there the conversation began.

They seemed nice people – if a little quiet – but the more they talked, the livelier they became. But it wasn't long before she began to feel like an alien in a foreign land. They were all full of opinions and most of them related to the people "out there" whom they often called "the lost."

They excluded Tanya from their views about those who didn't go to church, but she couldn't help feeling rather criticised and condemned anyway. She told herself inwardly that she'd wanted to know what they thought, but she couldn't help feeling uncomfortable.

It turned out that, though they knew it was their "Christian duty" to welcome outsiders in the chapel, they feared what it might do to their rather comfortable little club. These were some of the passing comments she picked out of their long conversation:

"We lay everything out for them out there and they don't come."

"When they do come, most of them don't stay."

"Those who do come, want to change things; we like things just as they are."

"But if people don't want to come to church, that's their disaster."

"Sometimes they sit in my seat!"

"I like worship as it is; I don't like happy-clappy" (Tanya had to ask them to explain this!).

"New things might not work, so we're better off staying the same."

"The old ones say that this chapel will see them out; we think we've got quite a good congregation these days. We'll be fine just with these people."

In the end, Tanya screwed up her courage and said she'd thought they were all just going through the motions when she'd been there last Sunday. Beth took great offence at that. She said, "We're all believers! We believe in God and that Jesus died for us. Just because we sit quietly doesn't mean we don't believe! Who are you to make that criticism? You've only been once!"

Tanya went red. "I just didn't feel there was much life around," she said.

"Typical! That's typical! What did you want? Happy-clappy?"

This seemed like a good moment to change the subject, which she managed to do successfully. Beth calmed down and the rest of the time was quite pleasant and Tanya hid the fact that she felt rather disturbed and emotional. They parted as seeming friends, though there was no reference to next Sunday's service or meeting again.

As she started home, she gradually collected her wits and in her usual strong-minded way, thought she'd try talking to the young man who had led the service. So she pushed Olly on a longish walk to the chapel and took down his address and phone number from the chapel notice board. She was nearly at the end of her tether, but she was determined to make one last effort.

The problem is...

We have amassed here a collection of very negative and misguided opinions. It's unlikely they'd all be found in one congregation, but we've heard them all expressed at various times – **have you?**

This is a congregation which seems to have lost its spark of life. It's perilously easy for any church to slip almost imperceptibly into the slough of dryness where people become frustrated and disappointed that those "out there" never come "in here." The point at which the people and/or the leadership begin to go through the motions is the point at which decay begins. Even a very large and apparently successful church isn't immune and can quickly slip into decline, so there's never any place for complacency in church life. When it becomes apparent that we've lost vision, purpose and have "a form of godliness but denying its power" 2 Timothy 3:5; where there seems to be scant evidence of the presence of the Holy Spirit and no spark of life, then the sort of situation we've described in the story can follow. If you see signs of such things in your church, it's time for urgent action!

Let us highlight some of the important questions**. Is this unhappy and ineffectual state the fault of the people, the pastor or a bit of both? What steps can they take to restore the presence of the Holy Spirit and a sense of purpose and mission? How can people be taught to look outward rather than inward? Are there simple activities which will lift people out of the slough of discouragement and restore optimism?**

As we analyse the church in the story in more detail, we can observe the following issues:

There's a complete lack of vision and adventure; risk and challenge. The people appear to be bored and have no sense that they're part of a movement which is trying to achieve something. So, they turn up on Sunday and go through the motions of worship, probably because they like to meet with their friends. This key issue for the fictional church in our story is revealed in the coffee shop where the three ladies talk about their "comfortable little club."

Maybe for some, Sunday attendance is merely a lifelong habit. Let's imagine that some people in the congregation are secretly rather frustrated with this, and, if they could be identified, could form a core for a leader to work with. There are weak leaders in every denomination but also frustratingly stubborn people**. If you are a leader facing a similar situation, can you identify some people with whom you could work to encourage change?**

The church in the story appears "dead," as in lacking a sense of the presence of God and evidencing little of the moving of the Holy Spirit. Spiritual life can only be stimulated by the spiritual activity of prayer. Lack of corporate, believing prayer in any church should be remedied urgently. An additional way to stimulate life is by a vigorous proclamation of the Gospel. It's always a huge encouragement for a congregation to know someone has given their life to Jesus. **When was the last time this happened in your church?**

Many of the people in this fictional church have a fear of doing new things and a resistance to change. They appear insular and parochial. This may be in their nature, or because they've not been shown any other way for a long time and have lost heart. Some in the congregation expect to be entertained in the way they like and leave it to the "professionals" to make things happen. Some could fear losing their security, so they cling to the familiar. The declaration, "we've never done it that way before" can be viewed either as resistance to change or an opportunity to change**. Change is always a challenge, but why does change matter?**

"Happy-clappy" is a dismissive term sometimes used to describe genuine Christians who like to express their worship that way. Christians who prefer lively worship could probably find very insulting terms for those who prefer a quieter expression of worship; they would be wrong to do so. We must stop the infighting. If we believe in the Gospel, then the rest is just personal preference.

The church isn't supposed to be a comfortable refuge away from a rapidly changing culture. There's a grave danger faced by both contemporary and traditional churches of closed friendship groups developing which make newcomers feel frozen out. It's especially in such closed groups that gossip and muddled ideas can multiply. Encouraging these groups to open up is a challenging task for any leader, but an essential task if the culture in church is to remain healthy. Christians must be prepared to be uncomfortable sometimes if they wish to grow the Kingdom of God; this is an inconvenient truth, but one which must be faced.

Some of the ladies' comments hint at an expectation that people will just show up in church, and, if they don't, it's somehow their fault. The great commission is a command for Christians to "go"; not a command for unbelievers to "come." People are generally consumers in our present culture, and, if there's nothing to persuade them to come or stay, they probably won't. These sorts of opinions seem to stem from a lack of vision which can lead people to feel frustrated and disappointed. We believe people can change their minds and hope that the church can grow and can be born in the heart. Appropriate vision which leads to action and success can turn most struggling churches around. So, the key task for a leader is to engage and inspire the present congregation. Though we reiterate, we have enormous sympathy for the leader who struggles to inspire people who are doggedly resistant to change.

Sometimes there can be a controlling spirit in a church which stems from a particular person or family. The only remedy for the leader may be to confront it head on. This can be costly and challenging if as a leader you are gentle by nature and find confrontation difficult. And you need to be sure that this is the case – it's sometimes difficult to assess.

Sometimes the leader can be controlling. There are many examples of controlling leaders whose "word is law" and know nothing about teamwork and empowering others. **Can you see any evidence of this in your church?**

When we stand before the Lord Jesus to give an account of our lives, and He asks us how we built His Kingdom, **what will we say?** "I didn't do much Lord; I just wanted it to see me out." What a selfish thing to say. **Could we truly look Jesus in the eye and say such a thing?** Yet you may have heard it said on numerous occasions. We know it's born out of a deep sense of disappointment, but it has no place in church.

The way ahead...

Good intentions aren't enough. Simply believing in Jesus isn't enough to grow the Kingdom of God. Most people in declining churches love Jesus but there must be good practice too. So, here are some suggestions for a leader and congregation caught in the lifeless situation that Tanya encountered. But beware: they involve change! And change is always difficult.

1. Develop a small team of key leaders to think through what the vision should be for the church. This group will often be a subgroup appointed by a church council or Parochial Church Council. It might be the eldership. Cast the agreed vision to the whole church and then begin to structure the church's activities to fulfil it. This might involve some drastic changes – which is why a team approach is always best.

2. Organise a challenging project which addresses a real issue of the day. Good examples include becoming a collection/distribution point for a food bank, starting a project to help homeless people, organising a befriending service for the elderly/ lonely, developing a book-lending library to replace the one which closed in town, opening a free café or providing free lunches for children during the school holidays. There are literally dozens of such initiatives and, if you visit the website of any large church, you'll find plenty of ideas to borrow and try. Find a person with a passion to lead this and develop a team around them. We emphasise again that such social projects must address a need that's very real in the community around the church and every opportunity to talk about Jesus should be maximised.

3. Make physical changes. This could be by altering the seating arrangements in church: let it face a

different direction, curve the seats, put seats around coffee tables, remove most seats if the congregation is small and sit in a circle. Alter the look of the building with decoration or wall murals. Create a mission team to lead the worship. Experiment with different worship styles, new songs and sounds. Preach a short message followed by discussion in small groups. Be prepared for people to find this unsettling.

4. Preach about the power of the Holy Spirit. There's some confusion about this in some Christian circles. Of course, we have the presence of the Holy Spirit. He is all around us, He was active in our lives when we found faith, we're "born again" of the Spirit and He resides within us. However, when it's recorded in Acts 1:8 that Jesus told the disciples to wait in Jerusalem for the Spirit, it wasn't for the presence but rather the power of the Spirit. The word for "power" in Greek is "dunamis" – it's the root of words like dynamite, dynamo and dynamic. It's a whole different level of experience. It's like the difference between the pilot light and full power of a central heating system – the light is always on but when the full power is kindled the whole house is warmed. Oh, how we need the full power of the Holy Spirit to energise our churches and equip us like He did those first disciples!

5. Encourage a few people to go on a retreat or conference such as Spring Harvest. They can return full of the power of the Holy Spirit and bursting with enthusiasm, which can result in a real injection of life into the congregation.

6. Pray for some new blood – some lively Christians to stir things up. Maybe a couple of Christian families could join your church and begin to set up some activities for children. **If there's a large church nearby, how about approaching them and asking them to plant a few families in your church?** This only works if you're welcoming and willing to change – they will most probably want changes in the style of worship, so be prepared!

7. Take some risks to break the attachment to the comfort zone. Explain what you're doing very thoroughly, giving lots of reasons why the change is necessary.

8. Make outreach your primary purpose – money, people and resources will follow. God is our provider, the ultimate faith-walker and He always responds when we step out in faith, as Hebrews 11 attests.

9. Organise a weekly prayer meeting to pray for the church and the community. This could be for an hour (or maybe only half an hour to begin with) in someone's home, or online (which post-Covid, has become more common). It doesn't matter if this is only attended by a few people because it will make an enormous difference. As the Bible says, the prayers of a righteous person are always powerful and effective (James 5:16).

10. Preach the Gospel regularly – sin, salvation, the cross, holiness and so on. Do this even if everyone in the congregation appears to have found Gospel faith. Some may not have, but the Lord will draw

people to hear the Gospel when He sees our commitment to share it.

11. The leaders could talk to people individually and try to change their thinking. Leaders should try to develop the art of persuasion. This should be done gently and thoughtfully, always taking care to listen. Trying to discover why people harbour negative thoughts can sometimes reveal past hurts, conflicts, disappointments and frustrations. This in turn can create opportunities for reconciliation and healing, which can totally transform the atmosphere in a church.

12. Leaders should visit all the people in their homes, with no agenda other than to share the love of Christ. This can be transformational.

13. Ask the people what they'd like to do to move their church forward. Implement some of the better ideas.

14. Multiple services are an obvious solution to irreconcilable differences between people's desire for traditional and modern forms of worship.

Questions for discussion...

We invite you to consider where the fault lies in the church we depict – with the distant, inexperienced and ineffectual leader or with the muddled, bored and stubbornly unfriendly congregation? If you're a leader, take time to examine yourself – do the same if you're a congregant.

Do you find that new people don't come to your church? Can you identify the reasons why?

Maybe visitors don't stay. Why do you think that is?

What changes need to be made to the culture of your church to make it healthier and more attractive?

As a leader are you guilty of simply marking time or are you putting your energy into driving things forward (see chapter 6)?

As a member of the congregation, are you merely content for the present style of church to "see you out?" Could you be persuaded to embrace change for the sake of future generations?

Do you need to pray for the power of the Holy Spirit?

Chapter Six
Leadership Matters

Tanya rang the front doorbell and waited patiently. In her usual single-minded way, she'd decided to tackle the young pastor who led the service on her recent church visit. She had many questions, so she'd discovered his phone number, rang him up and booked an appointment. He'd sounded very surprised on the phone but had covered it with politeness and patience. She was rather nervous, but very determined. Alfie was in a bad place about it all but had agreed to babysit for the evening. She was determined to bring this church adventure to a conclusion – satisfactory or otherwise.

The door opened. It was him: jeans and T-shirt, ruffled hair and quizzical smile. "Mrs Questor? Come in. Expecting you." He turned and she followed into a sitting room with a large settee and two lounge chairs. "Sit where you like," he offered. She sat on one chair, and he the other. "Now, how can I help you?"

"Well," she began rather breathlessly, "I was at your church last Sunday. You were at the front and I know you're the guy who's paid to do the work there, so I thought you were the best person to answer all my questions." Then she launched into a hurried description of the search she and Alfie had so far made to find a suitable church and all that had gone wrong. He remained quiet, until she started to describe her experiences the previous Sunday.

He was very apologetic, "Yes, I saw you there. We don't have many new faces – more's the pity. I'm sorry I didn't speak to you. I was caught up in another pastoral issue. What didn't you like about the service? I did my best."

"Well, I really don't know what I believe about Jesus and everything," she blurted out. I sort of expected there'd be some life and some passion in the people. They've been going a long time, so I thought I'd meet up with some of them. I just wondered what their view of everything was. They all seemed so defeated. They blamed everyone else for the state of the church, you know – no new faces and so on. They didn't really explain anything to me. What does it mean that Jesus died for us? I don't think you'll get people to come if they don't change their attitude. I'm sorry to be blunt, but they didn't seem any different from me. I expected their faith to sort of shine from them, but there was nothing there. Are all churches the same?"

"I don't know who you talked to, but it's a real struggle with this small congregation," he hesitated. "You seem like an intelligent woman. I'll explain a little, but please keep this to yourself. I'm a part-time pastor. I'm doing my training two days a week, and I've got another small church to look after too. It's the same atmosphere in both of them. My predecessor was elderly and retired on ill health grounds. I don't think he'd been effective for some years. He seemed to have given up. The people have lost morale. There are a few bright stars, but mostly they come out of habit, and I just don't know how to turn things around."

"They didn't even listen to you when you were speaking," she replied. "It all seemed a waste of time."

"I don't know whether I should say this, but that's how I often feel," he said. "You see, I'm living here by myself and unless my girlfriend comes around, there's no one to turn to and to discuss things with. She does her best, but she doesn't have a faith of her own and she thinks I'm wasting my time. I just don't know what to do to make any difference," he sighed. "This isn't helpful to you, I know. But there really isn't anyone to share with."

"Why don't you meet a group of them and try to find out ways you could change things. Maybe if you poke them a bit, they'll come out with some good ideas – you know? Like those bright stars you mentioned."

He looked at her hard. "I know what you mean, but I'm their leader, you see? It's up to me to come up with the bright ideas. That's what I'm paid for. I do believe in a team, but it's up to me to make decisions and then I'll put a team together to implement them."

"Well, Alfie and I are a team. We discuss what to do, we decide together and then we do whatever we've decided together. I think that's a team."

"Oh, you can't do that in a church," he shrugged. "You see, the people don't really know anything. I'm in charge and I have to set the direction. That's what I'm learning in my training. You see, there are some strong characters and I might not be able to control them if they come up with some ideas of their own. You'll keep our conversation to yourself?" he asked anxiously. "I don't think I should be talking to you like this."

"Can't you lead by example?" she asked. "If they see that you're determined and active, perhaps they'll follow – sort of copy you."

"I've got a lot on my plate: there's the training, looking after this house, visiting my parents and then there's my girlfriend. We're hoping to get married next year. I have to give her my time. This is a part-time job, so they tend to get a part-time commitment. I'm sorry, but that's the truth."

"But not all pastors will be like that, will they?" she asked innocently.

"What I know is that a lot of us have given up. We're just sort of going through the motions. A lot of church buildings are old and in need of repair. There's not much money around. And the church people have so many problems, that there's not much time for anything else. Of course, the building's not a problem in our place, but there are many issues to deal with. Don't think I'm not busy. There's so much to do that the weeks just fly past. It's difficult to get to grips with the community. We rarely get people from outside doing what you're doing, unless it's baptisms or weddings..." he paused, "...or funerals – they draw a lot in. However, the bereaved aren't in the mood for discovering more. In fact, they don't want to know about faith. They all have their own opinions – mostly those who are ignorant – and they're just not 'open.'" He rubbed his forehead in a worried fashion. "Sorry, this isn't helping you. I don't know whether we can help you. You can't expect much from the church people you met. They're not called to ministry like I am. They don't know much. The Lord is with them, but they're just volunteers."

Tanya didn't reply, but she thought, "Just volunteers! What about all those people who raise money for charity, who give so generously – just volunteers?" She liked the man, but she didn't like his attitude. He seemed to have stuff out of balance. And he seemed so defeated.

Suddenly he said, "I think you'd be better off finding another church. I don't think ours will suit you. But if you find one, you could come back here and talk to me about what you find. We could even talk through what Christians believe if you like." Just for a moment he seemed energised a little. Somewhere deep down within was a man who wanted to make a difference. He just seemed to have lost his way – as though the little chapel had burned nearly all his energy out of him. Yet, he was still so young – no more than his early thirties!

"There's a largish charismatic church on the main road about a couple of miles from here. They've a few hundred in the congregation and they're much livelier. I'd go there myself if I had the time. I've got the details somewhere on my desk." He meandered from the room, leaving Tanya to gaze around with her mind full of thoughts.

He returned quite quickly with a leaflet and passed it to her. It was colourful and garish and talked about miracles, healing and the Holy Spirit. There was a photo of a middle-aged man on the front, who was clearly the pastor and it was a sort of invitation to come and hear; come and see!

"You'll find life there," the pastor said as he led her to the door.

"Thank you for your time," she said politely, "and as for this – I'll pay them a visit and see if I can persuade Alfie to come. So, I might call on you again afterwards."

He shook her hand and she walked away thoughtful and just a little excited.

The problem is...

In this chapter we address the nub of the matter – leadership. It's our belief that wherever there's a growing church, you'll find an effective leader and in many declining churches there may be ineffectual leadership. We're aware that our example of poor leadership in this chapter is quite particular. We acknowledge that there are whole bookshelves full of worthy volumes about leadership and we could not possibly attempt to deal with the whole issue in this short chapter. We're trying to suggest some of the worst examples we've seen and some positive ways that leaders can improve their leadership techniques.

We highlight here some of the mistakes this young leader was making:

Our fictional young man was obviously a very fine person with good intentions and he wanted to share the Gospel. Regrettably, good intentions are never enough and he has lost his way, becoming disillusioned by what he sees as the stubborn intransigence of most of the congregation and their refusal to embrace his new ideas. **Do you think he is correct in this assumption?** We know of ministers who suffer ill health because they're constantly opposed and criticised by congregants. **Whose fault is this?**

The reader may observe that this fictional young pastor carelessly shared sensitive information about his congregation with a stranger. Maybe he needed somebody to talk to. Or was he just inexperienced? You might consider that he should've been more careful with what he shared with Tanya. **What do you think?**

The pastor mentions that he oversees two churches. The idea that a leader can effectively lead more than one church is, in our observation, a mistake (though we appreciate that in some circumstances there seems to be no alternative). We don't believe a leader can effectively lead and cast a vision for more than one congregation. Every church needs its leader to be present most of the time and where attention is divided, there's bound to be a deficit. Where a minister is given oversight of more than one church, we suggest that he/she tries to develop local lay leadership and/or leadership teams. There are encouraging signs in some denominations that this is beginning to happen. It takes time and effort to train and equip leaders but will be worth it in the long run, saving ministers from burn out and hopefully arresting the decline in congregations.

The pastor suggests he's overwhelmed by the scale of his task in bringing the church to life. However, it's absolutely the leader's role to change the atmosphere in a church in decline; not to accept the status quo. Of course, it may be that the leader joins a church that's already moving forward and developing. He needs to assess what, if anything, needs to change. Don't throw the baby out with that bath water.

Leaders are change makers: that's one of their primary functions. Our observation is that some denominations appoint too many people with strong pastoral skills as "leaders" but who actually have little or no leadership ability. This is a hard thing to say but we believe it to be true. It accounts for one of the main reasons why churches decline and ministers burn out. Leaders are movers and shakers, persuaders, influencers, team builders, organisers and vision casters. If a leader doesn't have these sorts of skills, they will tend to become a maintainer of what is, rather than a creator of what is yet to be. **Do congregations need pastoral care?** Of course! But sometimes this could be done by a pastoral team; leaving the leader free to drive the work forward. A true leader's mind will be haunted by visions of the future; big ideas and plans. Casting a vision involves simply explaining that picture of the future. Vision comes from God and is shared by a leadership team. An effective leader should explain this to the congregation and together with them devise activities to fulfil it. Churches are movements, not monuments. Standing still and marking time isn't an option because then a congregation will usually go backwards, and a leader's job is to push things forward and create momentum. A helpful illustration is that building a church is a bit like trying to walk up a downward-moving escalator: if you stop walking, you will go backwards. Walking up a downward-moving escalator is much harder work, but that is what is required to be an effective leader. However, we believe the Holy Spirit will bless a mission focus, and when a church begins to look outward, it will grow.

How can the leader engage with the "bright stars" in this church? Do you think this leader is doing any

leading or just showing up on Sunday and maintaining the present congregation? Where is his vision for the way forward? "I don't know how to turn things around," is a very honest admission. He seems to lack guidance and training in the practicalities of church leadership**. Do theological colleges offer too much theology and not enough practicality in their training programmes?**

The pastor complains he has no one to share with. **Does his church belong to a grouping of churches or a denomination? Could he develop a team within the church with whom he could confidently share his concerns and struggles? Could he find a mentor? Is there a pastor locally with whom he could pray and share; giving and receiving support, advice and encouragement?**

True teamwork isn't that the leader has an idea and gets others to implement it. Real team is a shared experience where an idea is arrived at corporately and implemented jointly. It's always the most effective way to work. This leader's idea of team is controlling and authoritarian which tends to demotivate people, especially professional people. It really isn't up to him to make all the decisions and there may be people in the congregation with better ideas than his. People with leadership potential in a church need to be given freedom and authority to lead or they will often leave. He said, "the people don't know anything" which is just plain wrong. A true leader's task is to unearth all the gems hidden in the congregation and help them to shine. Instead of trying to control strong characters, this leader should be trying to inspire them and release them to lead and then watch the church flourish**. If you're a leader,**

take a careful look at your attitude to others – do they threaten you?

Referring to unchurched people, the pastor said: "They're not open to finding out," but the opposite will be true in many cases and they will be curious if the Gospel is presented in an interesting, engaging and relevant way. If the love of Christ is offered to people outside the church, some will respond. **Do you think that some Christians have lost confidence in the power of the Gospel? How can this be remedied?**

It's a mistake to talk about "just volunteers!" There will be many in the congregation with more skills and life experiences than the pastor in many areas. No pastor is omnicompetent and those that think they are, are fooling themselves.

People need leadership. In the days of sailing ships, the sailors would "look aft" to judge the captain's mood – especially when they were sailing into danger. They would take courage from his calm demeanour and confident orders. We aren't suggesting that a leader should be like a captain in the sense of issuing orders, but that he/she should be present with the people, leading by example and word, attending events and encouraging teams because a congregation will "look aft"; it's human nature.

Has the pastor in our story had adequate training? Even where trainees are sent on placement, they can tend to learn the bad habits of existing weak leaders and so perpetuate the problem. In our view, ministers need an apprenticeship with a successful experienced leader to learn their trade. Just as apprentice joiners learn to work the wood and use the tools. There's a lot of practical skills that you can't learn from a book or from a lecture in Bible college – important though these are.

The way forward...

1. Lack of vision inevitably leads to the lack of a relevant programme which will build the church. There are leaders who have never conceived of vision casting. So, this is a crucial first step. Form a vision through prayer in concert with your leadership team and inspire your congregation with it.

2. Develop a pastoral team. Be patient and delegate responsibility. Truly delegate and try not to micromanage. Teams are king. It takes time and persuasive explanation to wean people off wanting the minister to visit and accepting that a visit from a member of the pastoral team carries equal weight. The effort is worth it in the long run because it will free you to concentrate on driving the church forward.

3. Visit some growing churches and talk to some effective leaders to learn new skills and borrow good ideas.

4. Always make a beeline for visitors to make them feel welcome.

5. Be an empowering, rather than a controlling leader. Take time to form a leadership team. A larger church needs a programme of training, forming and

releasing new leaders so they can take responsibility and then be set free to lead themselves.

6. Don't try to be a one person all-singing all-dancing leader. Empower others. Develop teams to run every area of church life.

7. Try to overcome your insecurity and take delight in the gifts and skills of others.

8. Don't let the church bullies and perpetual critics control the church: take charge. The leader must have a "firm hand on the tiller." This doesn't in any sense contradict point 5. Leaders should be engaged in building teams, empowering, equipping and releasing others; casting vision, teaching, persuading and encouraging the congregation. If there's someone else fulfilling this role, then there will be conflict and confusion.

9. **Is your leader burning out?** Get alongside him/her and offer some support. **Could you persuade him/her to share the load and develop some teams?**

10. Stop majoring on minors. Do not take six months of meetings to decide which colour to paint the hall. Separate the executive from the legislature. The legislature (PCC, Church Council etc.) should delegate and empower the executive (leadership team) to make decisions on practical matters and spend up to an agreed budget.

11. A leader must be a people person – able to offer some pastoral care, guidance, reassurance and encouragement; especially to visitors.

12. If you come to lead a church with no culture of empowering leaders, it's probably the work of ten to twenty years to create a new culture. So, take the long view.

13. The full-time paid professional and the lay Christian have equal ministries so remember to value everyone's contribution.

14. The leader should pay careful attention to developing their communication skills with their team, the congregation and the community at large. To be able to talk on a level with others and especially to listen to them, is an essential skill. There are many churches in the country which have learned to communicate brilliantly. **Why not go and visit them to see how they do it?**

15. Every church leader needs to develop a team who own the vision and share the load. Churches which have a minister attending only occasionally should be helped to develop a lay ministry. Every church should have a lay pastor where there isn't a full-time person who is responsible for leading the church forward and caring for the people. Such lay leadership can provide wonderful opportunities for people to exercise their leadership gifts (which they may employ in secular life).

16. If you're a leader, you may be thinking that you don't have the skills to do all the above. So, we would remind you that there are now many good courses available where you can receive ongoing training. Please search them out.

Questions for discussion...

In "The problem is" section above, we've included many questions for you to consider. Here are some additional ones:

If you're a leader, where do you come up short?

What steps can you make to improve?

If you're a member of a congregation, how can you support and encourage your leader in their difficult task?

Chapter Seven
Style Matters

A year had gone by and Tanya hadn't followed up on the suggestion made by the pastor. Her excitement had quickly faded when she got home to Alfie and described their conversation. He was quite cynical and thought that this "Rev" seemed more obsessed with his own life than he was in helping her. He beat down her every argument and persuaded her to give up the idea of finding a "perfect" church. So, she repressed her thoughts and feelings in the following months and concentrated on the needs of her career and the family.

But at the beginning of September, they were both diverted by the excitement of finding Tanya was pregnant again and so her concern about the needs of her growing family reasserted itself. One day, a few weeks before Christmas, a leaflet slipped through the letter box, just as colourful and garish as the one she'd seen in the pastor's house. This leaflet advertised the church he'd described as a "free" church and declared that it was to be visited by a famous American evangelist and healer. He was holding a series of meetings and the church was expecting to witness "awesome miracles of healing." This made her feel both nervous and excited. She showed it to Alfie. He was very dismissive, but he didn't want to upset his pregnant wife, so he promised to babysit so she could go to a meeting one Thursday night.

She had already sussed out the building, so she determined to arrive early and get a good seat. As she rounded the corner, she could hear loud and lively singing to the music of a band. "It's the warmup," she thought. She was used to gigs and concerts. The doors of the church were wide open and there was no entrance porch, so she slipped in at the back. The place was crowded and she was beckoned in by a man, who led her forward to sit on an empty chair by the aisle and next to the front row! She felt very conspicuous and self-conscious as she walked down, but didn't feel she could avoid his insistent and firm invitation to follow him and she sank down gratefully into her seat as the large band on the raised stage in front of her continued their enthusiastic music quite professionally, she thought. But what followed wasn't to her liking at all!

The "meeting" was introduced by a short, bald-headed man in jeans – he seemed to be in charge of the church and told a few "in jokes" that Tanya and many in the gathered audience didn't get at all. He gave a fulsome, but rather patronising introduction of the evangelist, whose name was Wilburt Groh. The aforementioned was a large, bulky man with shiny, spiky, blonde hair. It was clear that he worked out regularly: his T-shirt fitted tightly and made his rippling muscles obvious. He had a loud, deep laugh and seemed to thoroughly enjoy the proceedings. The band continued with more songs, lasting for fifteen or twenty minutes and Tanya felt the need to sit down part-way through. She was alarmed by the hand waving and flag waving. The flags were carried to the front and waved ecstatically, but not very carefully (several members of the audience on the front row were entangled and enveloped as the singing rose to a crescendo). Then the music stopped. Someone near the back began to speak out in a strange language. It sounded like, "Raise a *tum-tum*; grab a handhold; *wishy-washy ben amiti*," and so on. He was joined by others and large numbers of the congregation began to join in singing ecstatically and apparently in the same unknown language – hands raised in the air. Nobody explained what was happening and Tanya found it rather frightening. If she hadn't been near the front, she would've left at that point, but she was trapped by her own self-consciousness and she didn't want to make a scene. She could sense that a lot of the audience had become very expectant and excitable and wondered what was going to happen next.

When the bald-headed man called a halt to all this (by holding up his hand and shouting, "Stop! That's enough!"), a young guy, probably in his early twenties, got up and regaled the story of his life. Although he was American too and made many cultural references, she got it. "It's like going to a movie," she thought to herself. He was recently released from prison, he'd been in there because he'd funded his drug habit with a series of crimes. His story was the most interesting part of the evening. It held everyone gripped, although he didn't properly explain how his faith in Jesus had made all the difference. He quoted bits from the Bible, but didn't explain them, so the point of his story was wasted on Tanya. During the next few songs – and by now an hour and a quarter had passed – some of the audience became more ecstatic. The church leader interrupted them to say that a plate was being passed around for money. He encouraged people to "dig deep" to offset the costs of the "mission," as he called it. Tanya was embarrassed. She only had a pound coin with her and everyone could see what you put on the plate – there were many notes there. She wished she'd known in advance that she would have to pay for her night out and she thought it seemed a bit of a con in a "free" church!

Then the evangelist got up to preach. She'd heard one or two sermons by now – they'd been rather timid, slow moving and boring. This was completely different. Wilburt moved incessantly round the stage, waving his hands and arms around or chopping to prove a point. Sometimes he whispered so quietly even Tanya could hardly hear him and sometimes he shouted and pointed at different members of the audience very dramatically. His main theme was that if only the members of the audience – and Tanya herself – would give themselves over to Jesus, He'd bring them real prosperity. If they trusted Him, all their problems would go away and their illnesses would be healed. Tanya found it quite persuasive, but at the back of her mind was a nagging doubt. If everyone did this, then earth would be like Heaven, and she just couldn't see it happening.

The sermon lasted fifty minutes and the service's two-hour mark had been passed. Tanya thought Alfie would be getting worried. As the preacher came to his great climax, he finished with an appeal. He called for members of the audience to come forward for "salvation" and for healing, and they streamed forward in droves. They queued up to have hands laid on them and Tanya noticed that sometimes he pushed them hard; so much so that some of them fell over backwards and lay where they fell. One who was in the aisle waiting and in an excitable state, stumbled sideways even before he had been touched and fell into her lap. This was really the last straw. She pushed him off and climbed out of her seat.

She could tell that those members of the congregation still in their seats thought she was going to join the queue – they whispered together excitedly – but she was going in the other direction. With head held high, she made her way down the aisle, pushing past those still making their way down. She didn't know what to make of it all. She was confused and rather frightened. This was definitely not her cup of tea. What could she say to Alfie? She would have to confess to another failure. Of all the places she'd visited, this was the most alive, yet unquestionably the most disturbing.

It was yet another failure. She just couldn't find the place which spoke to her, answered her faith questions and made her feel that she'd found a community where her children could grow up safely. Where could she find this God these people seemed to believe in?

The problem is...

Here we're not intending to be disrespectful, but we're trying to describe this kind of meeting from the point of view of an unchurched person.

In his letter to the Corinthian church, St Paul encourages Christians to desire and express the gifts of the Spirit,

"Follow the way of love and eagerly desire gifts of the Spirit; especially prophecy." – 1 Corinthians 14:1

However, he also warns them to be careful that worship is conducted in such a way that unbelievers can be helped,

"What then shall we say, brothers and sisters? When you come together, each of you has a hymn or a word of instruction, a revelation, a tongue or an interpretation. Everything must be done so that the church may be built up. If anyone speaks in a tongue, two – or at the most three – should speak, one at a time and someone must interpret. If there's no interpreter, the speaker should keep quiet in the church and speak to himself and to God." – 1 Corinthians 14:26-28

Do your authors believe in exercising the supernatural gifts of the Spirit? Absolutely! But this needs to be done with caution in a public meeting. How to make the presence of God clear without alarming people is a crucial issue and it's not easy to do. The powerful presence of the Holy Spirit can be quite appealing to unchurched people who are genuinely seeking but if it's accompanied by weird or unusual behaviour it can sometimes be off-putting to them. It's a very difficult balance to maintain.

This type of service is absolutely not some people's cup of tea and there's no point trying to pretend otherwise. It's certainly true that no one style of worship will suit everyone. We suggest that this style of worship is clearly explained in advertising literature so that people know what they are coming to and can choose.

However, many historical revivals have exhibited this style of meeting. There are hints that in some early church meetings various charismatic phenomena were experienced. In some of John Wesley's meetings people would "swoon" or be overcome by the presence of God. Wesley sometimes even had water thrown on them to make sure they weren't faking (and in our present experience, we have observed people being pushed over but we've also seen people genuinely fall under the influence of the Spirit.)! Early accounts of Salvation Army prayer meetings contain descriptions of charismatic occurrences just like the ones described in our story. Yet in its day, the Salvation Army was incredibly successful in sharing the Gospel. Undoubtedly, this type of meeting has been the means of salvation for countless people. **How can we criticise it?** Such worship is very common in various parts of the world today – in places where the church is growing extremely quickly.

It's an empirical fact that there will always be a certain percentage of the population who will connect with this style and absolutely love it. They will be fascinated and challenged by the testimony which will give them hope. They will make a decision to follow Jesus there and then. If they're followed up and supported, they have a strong likelihood of becoming disciples. If supernatural healing does occur, interest in such meetings can explode, with people queuing around the block to get in.

So, let's analyse some of the mistakes:

Where was the ministry team to help people who "fall in the Spirit" and prevent them from hurting themselves or falling onto someone's lap? There should always be a team who assists the person praying, in order to help and support those receiving prayer (We append a list of dos and don'ts to help team members.).

Pushing is always wrong, because it's false. It's a human act (probably abusive) and not an act of the Holy Spirit. Whether people fall or not is irrelevant – some do; some don't. The issue for those who fall is whether they get up changed or whether they are acting or conforming to what they think is the accepted norm of behaviour in the meeting.

In a public meeting, speaking in tongues should always be explained, because unchurched people may find it scary or weird. In our experience a calm explanation will allay most people's fears and give the assurance that the meeting is being conducted in good order.

The front seats should always be occupied by regular members, leaving space for visitors to observe without embarrassment (This issue can be addressed in all styles of worship as we've illustrated earlier.).

There's some suggestion here that this particular evangelist over-egged the results of a newfound faith in Christ. It's not every Christian's experience that their new life in Christ brings them real success in life and freedom from sickness. Some of the most inspirational Christians (like St Paul himself) know hardship and persecution and their faith is honed through their experiences. Not every Christian is healed and we will all die one day. Real faith faces such obstacles with courage and devotion and many of the saints of the church, known and unknown, faced suffering with equanimity, and were and are a guide and example to others.

The meeting was far too long. Singing endless choruses isn't helpful to visitors, nor is an overlong sermon. It can be a peculiarity of this type of worship that it falls into a kind of "free church liturgy" – choruses, tongues, more choruses, testimony, offering, message and response. Always the same. Yet it's billed as "free worship" which is supposed to contrast with worship using a prayer book.

Sometimes we can become so immersed in a style of worship we like, that we can't see ourselves as others see us!

What appears to be "weird stuff" can be very off-putting for unbelievers – flag waving, dancing, hand-raising, shouting out, laughing, rocking, falling, pushing, running about – we've seen it all. **Is there a place for two acts of worship: one for seekers and one for believers?** Often loved and well-attended though they are, this style of service can confuse and even scare unbelievers.

Repetitive singing can put people off; especially men. "Jesus is my boyfriend" type songs put some men off because they are perceived as being too girly. **Do you think that matters?**

The way forward...

1. Have some seats set aside at the back for first-time visitors and late-comers.

2. Cut down the length of the meeting, sing fewer songs and ditch some of the very repetitive choruses.

3. Advertise the service clearly – what it will be like and then have an alternative service which is more accessible for unchurched people who would like a different style.

4. Carefully (and regularly) explain everything that is unusual; such as tongues or falling.

5. Preach a much shorter sermon – attention spans are getting shorter. The testimony was powerful, so only a brief explanation of the Gospel may have been necessary.

6. Never push people over. If God wishes to move in this way, He will, without any help from us.

7. Have a well-trained ministry team available (see Appendix 2) who also have a clean DBS and have attended safeguarding training.

8. Try to vary the meetings so they don't fall into a pattern.

9. Make sure that everything that happens is a genuine move of the Holy Spirit and not contrived or exaggerated, because people will quickly suss this out.

Questions for discussion...

The big issue for leaders is that if God can choose to move in this way, how can that be effectively managed without quenching the Spirit?

In our depiction we try to illustrate that the problem isn't with the moving of the Holy Spirit in the meeting – God's part – but with the human element. So, we pose a key question: Is this service contrived and over-ecstatic? **Have you been to meetings which left you cringing and confused? Is that your fault or theirs?**

Chapter Eight
Success (Matters)!

Good stories need to have a happy ending and this is no exception. Six years have passed. Ollie is now seven and Bridge (Yes, Bridge!) is five. There's been no contact with any church in the intervening period, but their bad experiences continue to haunt Alfie and Tanya. Was there somewhere something of reality in the midst of all the ecclesiastical mess? In case you, dear reader, are feeling a little depressed about what they've found (or haven't found) of Jesus in their locality, here are five alternative happy endings (They only did one of these – so, take your pick!) to give you hope for the future. We want to emphasise that we depict here only five happy endings but acknowledge that there are many other styles of church which can prove attractive to unchurched people.

Cathedral.

The family were spending the weekend with relatives in a large and prosperous, rather middle class, cathedral city – you know, that sort of touristy place with living museums, up market restaurants and bars and tiny little coffee (and cream tea!) shops. Tanya and Alfie left their two children in the care of their doting aunt and went for a stroll in the early afternoon sunshine, in the leaf-dropping early autumn. The cathedral with its soaring spires dominated the skyline, and its historical fascination that brought it many visitors daily.

As they passed by the entrance to its large, open front square, Tanya glanced at Alfie. "Shall we?" she whispered, "Just to see the sights?"

He shrugged. "Just a one-off?"

"Yes – just a one-off" and she took his hand and led him to the front porch, following a stream of interested visitors.

As they passed into the interior, their mood of gaiety faded, to be replaced by a sense of awe. There were many people walking around the vast space, but they were all either silent or talking in hushed tones. The cathedral soared above them. They craned their necks to see the vaulted ceilings, the magnificent stonework, and the fluted pillars that supported this incredible vastness. A friendly woman welcomed them, offered a guided tour, which was starting from the entrance in the next few minutes and, as an alternative, pointed out some of the places they might like to visit within the cathedral's environs.

For the first time, Alfie felt the sense of a presence outside himself; something above and beyond and out there. He surprised himself when the words "good" and "holy" came into his mind. There was a small gift and bookshop just across from the entrance and Tanya slipped in to buy a simple guidebook. They turned down the tour and followed the map, reading a mixture of history and theology as they strolled round together. The book was well written and explained in simple terms the purpose of the cathedral, its heritage and history and its attempt to lead people to an experience of God, a living faith, as well as its service to the community in the twenty-first century.

As they neared the nave, the quiet singing they had heard as they entered grew louder. There was a robed choir in the choir stalls, young and old, male and female, singing a song of glory to God. Neither of them knew the melody, but they loved the perfection of the harmonies and sat down in a pew to listen. Somehow it matched the surroundings and it gave them both this sense of "other" outside themselves. Tanya felt shivers run up and down her spine. She just had this sense that there was something more, something ethereal, beautiful, beyond their usual humdrum existence. Then they realised they were in a service. They heard the Bible read in plain, modern English and short, meaningful prayers, which somehow brought them closer to the One who lay beyond. It was a significant half hour and when choristers and readers had withdrawn, they both sat for a few minutes savouring the silence.

"This is what I've been looking for," Tanya whispered and Alfie nodded.

"It's something..." He couldn't put it into words, "it's something we need. We must come again. Perhaps He is out there somewhere."

Questions for discussion...

Do you think that their previous experiences of church had left a legacy in their minds?

What other seeds had been sown, even though those experiences were often negative?

What do you think Gospel seeds are? Why did the words "good" and "holy" pop into Alfie's mind? Where did they come from?

Attendance at cathedrals in Britain is on the increase; why do you think this is so?

How would a cathedral's pastoral team notice people like them, so that they could be welcomed, included and brought into the family of the cathedral church?

The cathedral was obviously very well organised; why is this important?

Beautiful places and glorious music can bring us closer to God. Why is this so?

Café Church.

Tanya helped Ollie to complete his crude drawing of a Roman soldier. She had control of the paper scissors and she cut round the edges of the red tunic he had designed on sticky paper – the next stage was to dress their artistic creation and give him a sword. Ollie was totally absorbed in the activity, as were the other small children sitting at the round table beside him. The mothers too were enjoying themselves. There was a scattering of artistic materials in front of them, as was true at the other tables in the large civic hall. The children were shortly to leave for their age-related activities in the adjoining rooms, as their parents were to listen to a lively but simple explanation of one of the parables of Jesus, illustrated on the screen in front of them.

Tanya had been bringing Ollie and Bridge on a Sunday morning for some weeks. She had heard about it through another mum who attended a lively modern church in the next town. They had met when they were both expectant mothers and had maintained the friendship since, even though they lived a few miles away from one another. When the church her friend attended decided to plant into the community building in Tanya's hometown, her friend had kept her posted. Tanya had gone with some apprehension, but had received a warm welcome and liked the informal style of the set-up. They called it "Café Church," and after the talk they'd indeed drink coffee and eat cakes – sometimes made by the parents who attended and on this particular day Tanya had made a large fruit cake. While they ate, they talked informally about what they'd heard and Tanya found that as the weeks went by, she was beginning to understand about this Jesus in whom Christians believed so passionately. She had made good friends. She had lost her nervousness and shyness and felt completely at home. In her one-to-one chats with one of the leaders, he had described the event as a messy church for the kids and café church for their parents or people responsible.

"It's our latest idea," he said. "Only an hour and a quarter, but catering for adults and young children alike. We have other activities starting for the older ones and Ollie and Bridge will be welcome at these as they grow older."

Tanya found that the family were not ready to go for at least half an hour after the event had ended – the children played (usually happily) and the grown-ups chatted together. She found the whole morning really uplifting and was beginning to find her way to faith. She had already been invited to lunch with some of her new-found church friends and she and Alfie had gone along to a couple of barbecues the church had organised. She was thrilled when her husband had declared he enjoyed them. She hoped that one day she'd be able to persuade him to come along to the main event.

Questions for discussion...

Why are activities for children so important?

Why do you think unchurched people need simple explanations of Biblical stories?

Why are screens helpful in our culture?

People can form friendships through shared experiences like pregnancy. How can people in your church link with people through some shared activities and interests?

Why is friendship a vitally important tool for building church?

Why is informality helpful for many people in today's culture?

Jesus often engaged with people over meals. Why is food important? Could you use food in your church to attract people and help them develop friendships?

Why is it necessary to talk about Jesus, as well as helping people?

The Christians at this café church are building as they go, starting small but with plans for the future as children grow up. What plans could you make to grow your church?

Traditional Church.

As Ollie had grown, Tanya had become more concerned about finding him good friends who would lead him in the right direction. She was trying to teach him right from wrong, even though she was a little unsure herself. However, she wanted him to get the best influence. His school was good and Bridge had settled down well there too, but some of the kids Ollie played with were rather wild and she still had this idea, perhaps mistaken, that if she could find the right church, the environment would act as a positive balance for him.

There had been a long gap of six years since her last unfortunate experiences, but she decided to take her courage in both hands and try again at their local church – she had heard that a new "rev" was now in charge and hoped that things may have changed. So, one Sunday she left the kids with Alfie and slipped along to the large grey building with a spire, with its doors now wide open to admit a reasonable stream of people of all ages; families included. The pews had been replaced with comfortable seats, there was carpet on the floor and she noted with relief that there was only one book tucked into the shelf attached to the chair in front of her.

The experience that followed was so different from that of years ago. This was definitely a family affair. Nobody played the organ, there was a small band and the songs appeared on the screen over the altar. The young clergywoman who led the service seemed totally aware of the presence of first-time visitors and explained everything clearly. She explained the use of the book for read prayers, gave a lively little talk for the children and her sermon was clear and professionally illustrated on the screen. Tanya enjoyed it all and was glad to see a few children of around the age of her own; fully engaged in the service. It only lasted fifty minutes and was followed by refreshments, served from the back of the church. Several people around Tanya's age engaged her in conversation and she found that some families had only been coming a short time. The town grapevine had passed on the changes being made, and to be made and these suited her ideas of what church and worship should be.

The "rev" moved over to speak to her and Tanya found her relaxed and easy to talk to. She found she could ask the question that had crossed her mind previously. It was about having her children baptised. She knew they would be older than the norm, but this engaging young woman saw no problem in that and agreed to meet with Tanya and Alfie to talk further. Tanya hesitated a little before she dared tell her about their previous bad experience, but the reverend was so friendly and this was such a warm family atmosphere, that she found herself opening up, particularly about Alfie's disappointment and cynicism. Rachel (as she had introduced herself) listened carefully, asked one or two perceptive questions and then suggested that she would call round, ostensibly to meet her and discuss baptism at a time when Alfie would be there, so that she could be introduced. She told her that the church was now running a series of activities particularly for enquirers and that she would try to slip these into her conversation with Alfie. She also said she would pray for them as a family. Tanya was elated. It might work, it might not, but it was the first positive step forward for many a year. She left the church determined to bring her children the following week.

Questions for discussion...

What positive changes had the new reverend made? Why are these changes so helpful for an unchurched family?

What leadership skills did the new reverend have that the previous one didn't? Do you think these skills could be learnt?

How could you develop a "warm family atmosphere" in your church?

Why is prayer an important ingredient in church growth?

Bounce in the House.

Alfie had become a fitness fanatic. He had joined a local gym and went three times a week, once very early in the morning, once after work and once at the weekend. His fitness instructor had initially given him an introductory programme and he had moved on from this to other programmes for a year or so, until he'd been introduced to a personal trainer, who had given him an introductory free personal training of one hour. He loved it! Ten sessions were expensive, but he saved for them and gained much from them. He then felt able to design his own programme for toning and fitness and followed it religiously. In fact, it would be fair to say that attending the gym regularly had become his religion. He added to his tattoos and drank loads of protein shake. He didn't want to bulk up at first, but he quickly became addicted in the same way as many gym members and he noticed the difference hugely in his personal appearance and physical ability. It did a lot for him mentally too and he became much more positive in his view of life.

But one evening after work he had an unfortunate accident in the gym. He was tired, and a heavy barbell slipped from his grasp. He tried to catch it, and in so doing, pulled something in his back, as the barbell clattered to the floor. He cried out in pain and a young guy who had been doing some kettlebell exercises, put them down and rushed over to see if he was OK. Alfie was away from the gym for a couple of months while he had physio and rested, but he and this young guy became friends and met at the pub several times. Alfie discovered his mate was a Christian who went to a large church based in a unit on an industrial estate nearby. So, as he had to lay down temporarily his gym religion, he decided, when invited, to have a go at that religion he had rejected bitterly some years ago. It wasn't just because he was invited, but because he was called for and he and Jake went together. Jake was relaxed when he made his invite and said he was sure Alfie would get as much out of it as he did. Alfie himself knew it was going to be similar to a secular gig and had once caught a glimpse of songs delivered in that style when Tanya had been watching "Songs of Praise" and he had grudgingly admitted to himself that he had quite liked them.

There were hundreds of people, mostly young, gathered in the industrial unit and the bounce was definitely in the house. A vast screen, a rock band, stage lights, movement, excitement, laughter and all focussed on Jesus. He was sucked into the atmosphere, in one way so familiar to him and everything that was said – relevant, modern, clear and pointed – spoke directly to his mind and heart. He knew he had found the "church" that suited him. After the meeting, Jake introduced him to a group of men who were into motorbikes, as he was and all of them Christians. As they shared their stories of how they had found faith, he began to open up. In the weeks following, he brought Tanya and the children. They all found it fun, but they liked it most because it was real and spoke to them. It wasn't long before the whole family, each at their own level, had placed their trust in this Jesus in whom their new-found church and their new-found friends, so fervently believed (Yes, even Bridge.).

Questions for discussion...

In the Gospels it's recorded that Jesus mostly met people on their turf (but only occasionally in the synagogue or Temple). Why is it necessary for Christians also to meet people on their own ground – both in their culture, as well as in their place?

Why is personal testimony so powerful?

Believers who have been trained in personal witness can become much more effective. Could you organise some training in your church? It can be helpful to write your testimony down and hone it, learn it and be ready to share it.

Are you looking for opportunities to share Jesus?

Do you think that we need a variety of different church styles to meet the needs of people in our society? Should we be encouraging one another, rather than criticising each other (as sometimes happens)? Why?

Contemporary Church

"Turn out the light!" Alfie sounded annoyed. It had been a long day at work, and he knew that Bridge was likely to interrupt their sleep. Tanya smiled, put her book down and flicked off the switch by the side of the bed. She'd just been reading the Parable of the Sower. She'd found the right church at last. She had Googled for local churches and this one had a really lively and interesting website. So, she took the kids by bus to the south of the town and found it. It was just what she was looking for – modern, informal, friendly.

She had been reminded of the church she'd visited when the American evangelist came to town. It had many of the same characteristics – a praise band, a riveting story of someone's life and faith, hand and flag waving, an emphasis on the Holy Spirit, song and spoken tongues, but everything was simply explained before, during, or after it happened, so she didn't feel alarmed or frightened. She was able to observe what was happening around her – what was real, and what was false. She liked it. She liked the sense she had of a Presence beyond herself, beyond all other people, something she called "warm and shivery."

So, she'd gone again – and again, and again. There was a crèche for Bridge and there were children's activities for Ollie. They were happy and settled. She'd told Alfie all about it and he'd got used to his family going there every Sunday, though he himself didn't have the same inclination.

As she grew in understanding, her faith grew. And then one Sunday she had this experience of God that He loved her and was close to her and she invited Him and His Holy Spirit to enter her life. She had begun again. And the world looked different and she felt transformed, cleansed. In her new life she was supported and encouraged by her church friends. She felt really happy. There were, of course, many problems and issues for her – life was like that. But she was beginning to learn how to find her way through them with the Holy Spirit's help. The church had shown her how He was always with her, in a gentle way – supporting, consoling, guiding.

She was filled with delight as she turned over in bed. He was real. It wasn't just about finding somewhere that inculcated morality into her two children. She now wanted them each to find Him in their own time – and Alfie too! But she knew how hard it was to convince anyone else that what she was experiencing daily was for them too. She would encourage Alfie, she thought and would pray for him until she persuaded him to go to experience this lively, Spirit-filled, sane and sensible worship, so he could find his own way through it to a living experience of his own. She said her prayers for Alfie, Bridge and Ollie with her eyes closed and then drifted off into a dreamless sleep.

PHILIP BARBER AND BRIAN BARBER

Chapter 9
Final Thoughts

We hope you've found this book thought-provoking and challenging. Perhaps it's been rather painful in places. We reiterate that we've never intended to be overly critical or unkind, but to help people analyse how they can better grow the Kingdom. We'd rather be cast in the role of a physician making a series of diagnoses which we hope might eventually lead to the cure of a very sick patient. We want the church to awaken from its slumber!

In Revelation 3 there's a letter to the church in Sardis. Verses 1-2 say:

These are the words of Him who holds the seven spirits of God and the seven stars. I know your deeds; you have a reputation of being alive, but you are dead. Wake up! Strengthen what remains and is about to die, for I have found your deeds unfinished in the sight of My God.

These words could very well apply to many churches in the Western world. It really is time to wake up and strengthen what remains, before it dies.

Your authors have both spent the better part of their lives trying to grow the Kingdom and we've made many mistakes along the way, so we join with you in the struggle of trying to be more effective. It's the passion we have for God's church that caused us to write this book. We believe in the power of the Gospel to change lives and transform communities and whole countries. The Church need not die, it can be reborn, but we must awaken from our slumber!

Some Christians rather naively say: "We're waiting for revival" or "Revival is about to happen." They've been saying that for all the years we've been in Christian service and it hasn't happened. We need to talk less about revival and set about revival! While some Christians seem to be waiting for a move of God, He's waiting for a move of people. He has already moved two thousand years ago and He's always moving as He chooses.

It's certainly very true to say that we need to get back to preaching the plain Gospel, but you can preach all you like to an empty church and no one will become a disciple of Jesus Christ. We hope through this book you can see that there's much more to it than that – unless we present and explain the Gospel in accessible ways, there won't be any new Christians.

Successfully growing the Kingdom of God involves a complicated cocktail of ingredients. The recipe will vary a little from situation to situation and among different people groups. No one size ever fits all. But the cocktail will always include ingredients like good leadership, clear strategy, teamwork, quality, clarity, friendship, relevant preaching, love, planning, programming, vision casting, intentionality, prayer, the power of the Holy Spirit and effective cultural language – to name but a few. We hope you can glean many ideas from the pages in this book.

As we've said, churches are movements not monuments, so change is a constant. Change is also a dirty word in some quarters, but, as society continues to advance, change must occur. In previous generations, the church was at the forefront of innovation and led the predominant thinking of the age rather than trying to ape it. We hope the present church can regain the initiative.

One definition of insanity is doing the same thing over and over again and expecting different results. If this is a truism, why do we persist in doing the same things in church hoping things will get better? We emphasise that the change we're talking about is largely concerned with methods rather than theology. We believe that the unchanging Gospel can be dressed in new clothes to make it accessible to our time. Such churches exist – and they are growing.

If you're a leader, we wish you success in the awesome task to which you've been called. If you're a follower, please support your leaders and be part of the team – join in and share your gifts and expertise. Together we can continue the great adventure in building the Kingdom of God in our time.

This is a call to arms! Are you up for the challenge?

Appendix 1

Some Ways to Help Keep a Conversation Going.

"Hello, it's lovely to meet you, I'm (name). What's your name?"

If there are children, ask their names and greet them and maybe make a friendly comment or question e.g. "I bet you're glad it's school holidays," or "What did you get up to yesterday?" (Assuming it was Saturday.)

"Can I get you a cup of tea or coffee?"

"Have you travelled far? Do you live nearby?"

"Do you know anyone here?"

"Have you been part of another church?"

"What kind of week have you had?" Chat about your week too.

"What do you do in your spare time?" Tell them something about yourself. Try to find an area of mutual interest to converse about.

"Share a couple of things about the church, e.g. 'The service starts at…it's usually around an hour… it's quite informal… there's kids work/crèche… the conveniences are over there…'"

"Is there anything else you'd like to know?"

"Can I introduce you to…?" (Think of linking them with someone who has similar interests or if they have children, link them up with the children's leader etc.)

"I hope you enjoy your time with us."

If in a large church, never say: "Is this your first time?" Instead say, "I don't think I've spoken to you before." Thus avoiding a potentially embarrassing moment which can undermine all your efforts to create a welcoming experience.

Appendix 2
Response Teams

We recognise that the vast majority of churches don't have ministry or response teams. These are teams that deal with an invitation to come forward for prayer, commitment, healing, difficult issues and so on. Many churches, however, have places for private prayer and we recommend that these are made available to individual worshippers before or after each service – even during, if necessary. If you have no such small chapel or area, we recommend that you create one.

We further suggest that it's helpful for a ministry or response team to be available at each service if needed. A small group of such prayerful and committed Christians could then offer support to those coming to faith or seeking God's guidance in their everyday lives. There's also a real place for prayer for healing.

This appendix seeks to give guidance on how a response team might operate effectively. If presently your church gives no opportunity for response, why not consider engaging in this particular ministry?

All Christians believe that the Holy Spirit is active in the world, the church and the individual. When you become a member of a ministry team, you must be prepared to open yourself to the activity of the Holy Spirit as a channel from God through you to the person for whom you are praying.

Response Team Training

1. Objectives

a) Try to show Christian love to those to whom you minister.

1 Corinthians 13:1-2

If I speak in the tongues of men or of angels, but do not have love, I am only a resounding gong or a clanging cymbal. If I have the gift of prophecy and can fathom all mysteries and all knowledge, and if I have a faith that can move mountains, but do not have love, I am nothing.

b) Become a channel for the Holy Spirit so that He might minister to the person.

John 7:38-39

'Whoever believes in Me, as Scripture has said, rivers of living water will flow from within them.' By this He meant the Spirit, whom those who believed in Him were later to receive. Up to that time the Spirit had not been given, since Jesus had not yet been glorified.

A team member will thus try to accomplish the following:

- Facilitate the moving of the Holy Spirit under the direction of the pastor or other appointed leader.

- Help to avoid confusion, harm or offence.

- Release God's love, healing and encouragement to those who indicate a desire for prayer.

- Edify, exhort and comfort.

- It's not the purpose of this ministry team to rebuke, correct or give direction.

- It's not the purpose of this ministry team to provide counselling or any other in-depth ministry.

2. Personal preparation

It's important to be prepared by endeavouring to develop your own spiritual life through regular prayer, worship and Bible study.

3. When there's an invitation to come forward for prayer (or remain behind etc.):

- Listen carefully to the minister.

- Move forward if required or wait until the end of the service.

- Equip yourself from a box provided by the church which should contain a lanyard and supporting booklets etc.

-

4. When an invitation comes for a decision to follow Jesus:

a) Select a same-sex responder.

b) Take them aside.

c) Ask them to confirm their decision.

d) Pray a prayer of commitment with them. What is required is a prayer in which they repent of past failures, commit themselves to Jesus and ask Him to come and live in them.

e) Explain that we each need to grow as a Christian disciple and this is facilitated by regular prayer, Bible study, fellowship, worship and by endeavouring to witness to others and serve Christ in the World.

f) Fill in a response form if permitted to do so (This simply records a person's name and contact details.).

g) Give them supporting materials such as first Bible study notes, etc.

5. Other invitations to come forward

a) You should come forward either during or at the end of the invitation as appropriate; work in pairs – a mixed sex pair is preferable.

b) Smile, introduce yourself and ask the responder's name.

c) Ask what they would like prayer for. Do not get involved in their life history.

d) Encourage the responder to relax and, if helpful, to hold out their hands to receive.

e) Pray only for a minute or two and then move on.

f) Try to pray very simple prayers.

g) Remember, this isn't a counselling situation.

h) Elderly or disabled people should sit.

i) Under eighteen year old individuals should always be accompanied by a responsible adult.

6. General points

a) Touching

When you're praying, do not touch the responder – unless to lay hands on a head/shoulder, but you must ask permission to do this.

b) Occasionally people might fall over.

Be prepared for this by ensuring there's someone else nearby (of the same sex) who is prepared to catch them. Keep your eyes open when you pray.

c) We pray in FAITH

If a person shows no outward signs of being healed or touched by the Holy Spirit, this doesn't mean that they aren't.

d) Personal Issues

Pay attention to personal hygiene and wear modest clothing.

e) Get Help

If a situation arises that you feel you can't handle, get help immediately.

f) Respect

People are always to be treated with respect.

g) Confidentiality

Maintain strict confidentiality unless a responder begins to disclose a situation of abuse and you consider that this might be a safeguarding matter – stop them and explain that according to law you may be required to report to the authorities.

h) Personal Space

Respect personal space. Sit or stand to the side.

7. Praying for people at other times than at the end of church worship (e.g., the home, hospital, hospice etc.):

a) For your own personal safety, you should always let someone else know when and where you are going.

b) Men should be visiting and praying for men; women for women.

c) The same guidelines about not touching, never pushing, safeguarding, respect etc. apply in the home or hospital.

d) Always pray before you visit, asking God to make you a blessing and encouragement.

e) Always ask if you can pray; don't make any assumptions and always ask what they want prayer for.

f) Always be sensitive to the person and their situation.

g) It's usually helpful to read a few uplifting verses of scripture with them before praying.

h) Keep the prayer short.

i) Sometimes people need additional support, counselling or advice; in which case it would be best to refer them to a pastor/minister etc.

j) Additional points in hospital situation:

- Be courteous and respectful to professional staff always.

- You may have to pray silently if staff or relatives are present.

- Be prepared to wait if the person is being attended to.

Appendix 3
Personal Evangelism

A primary aim of each Christian is to help others discover faith in God, Father, Son and Holy Spirit.

It's easy to determine when something is on fire. It ignites other materials. Any fire that doesn't spread will eventually go out. A church without evangelism is a contradiction in terms; just as a fire that doesn't burn is a contradiction.

In Luke 7:36-50 we read about the occasion when Jesus had dinner at Simon the Pharisee's house and a "sinful" woman came in and anointed His feet with perfume – much to Simon's indignation. We highlight three things that this story teaches us about Jesus' approach to evangelism:

Firstly, we should try to get out of the ghetto (By which we mean the cloistered church environment.)!

Jesus went willingly into a hostile environment. We know it was hostile because Jesus reveals that Simon hadn't extended to him any of the courtesies normally expected when a Rabbi visited your house. There seems to be the implication that Simon was being deliberately discourteous or perhaps he was testing Jesus to see how He would react.

Jesus went to people even at some personal cost. He met unbelievers where they were. He realised what many Christians today still don't seem to understand: Farmers must get out into the field. According to one count, the gospels record one hundred and thirty two contacts that Jesus had with people. Six were in the Temple, four in the synagogues and one hundred and twenty two were out with the people in the mainstream of life. If all our spare time is spent in church, how can we ever hope to tell someone about Jesus?

A man once testified in one of D.L. Moody's meetings that he had lived "on the Mount of Transfiguration" for five years. "How many souls did you lead to Christ last year?" Moody bluntly asked him. "Well," the man hesitated, "I don't know." "Have you saved any?" Moody persisted. "I don't know that I have," the man admitted. "Well," said Moody, "we don't want that kind of mountaintop experience. When a man gets up so high that he cannot reach down and save poor sinners, there's something wrong."

Christians – we must get out of the ghetto. We must try to put ourselves in situations where we can make friends with people who don't know Jesus.

How about joining a local club or volunteering at a community project where you can make friends and look for opportunities to chat about your faith? It can be so easy to share Jesus.

Secondly, don't look for personal acceptance – just share Jesus.

Jesus was always true to Himself and to His principles. He taught people to love their neighbours and here we see Him doing just that despite the disapproval and social pressure of the people around Him. He allowed the woman, who was a prostitute (a sinful woman), to anoint His feet knowing full well that Simon would disapprove. For a respected Rabbi to allow such a woman to touch him was shocking and probably unheard of in that society. Jesus didn't seem to care if people approved of Him, liked Him or accepted Him. He cared about the woman more than He did His personal approval ratings. **Can you see how great the love of Jesus is for one poor sinner?**

We think this issue is a big challenge for us when we mix with people and make it plain that we follow Jesus. Some people will reject us. Well OK; so they will. Take it on the chin. Accept it as part of the territory. Jesus did. Don't be obsessed with wanting to be liked by everybody. Be true to the faith which is in your heart. Stand up for your convictions. If someone rejects you because of your faith, love them anyhow!

Notice that Simon was hostile to Jesus, but the woman was seeking. We suggest that for every hostile person, you'll find many more who are genuinely interested. Just sow your seeds about. Let Jesus gently ooze out of the pores of your life as you meet people and make friends. God will use your seeds in ways you don't expect.

Thirdly, tell them about Jesus.

Notice also that Jesus personally led this woman to faith. She found her way forward through the loving acceptance offered by Jesus, but He also took time to talk to her, to explain things and lead her to believe in Him. Why do we say: "Believe in Him?" Because He said: "Your sins are forgiven," thereby claiming God's authority for Himself. We hope you understand what we are saying here that people come to faith through believing in Jesus. As it says in Acts 4:12, "*Salvation is found in no one else, for there is no other name under heaven given to men by which we must be saved.*"

So, the aim of our evangelism is to talk about Jesus; to help people to think about Him and to share what we have found in Him.

To be a nice, kind person is, well, nice, but it's not enough. There are plenty of nice people about. Just to invite people to church or the youth group is good, but it's not enough.

It's not enough for people to say, "Oh, she's a nice person. I think she goes to church." "He's good; he's religious."

People generally won't come to faith just because of our good deeds. We have got to talk to them. We have got to look for little opportunities to slip into the conversation, something which will get them thinking about Jesus. Maybe if they confide in us, we could offer to pray for them. When you have that sort of conversation where you are "putting the world to rights," for example, you have your big opportunity to slip in what you believe about Jesus.

You could always try the direct approach. You might be surprised at how many people in our society are open to a direct conversation about Jesus. Of course, how you approach this task isn't easy. You aren't called to be a "Bible basher"; a bore who can talk of nothing else. The opportunity to speak about Him usually comes within a developed relationship. We don't love people and make friends with people, in order to feed them the Gospel. We befriend them, we love them for their own sake and for what friendship and love they offer us in return. One of the joys of this life is the loving friendship we can find wherever we go and in whatever we do – it does of course stem from Him – and it's His love for His creation flowing through us. But the very best thing we can do for them is to introduce them to Jesus. So, we need to choose our moment carefully when we sow that seed. It often comes from questions asked about our lifestyle and our beliefs, because our friends, our loved ones, have noticed something in us, and they are curious to know what it is. Our response will be measured and just the right length – an ability that comes from a lifetime's experience and quite a few failures. It's usually helpful to the other person not to labour the point or push for response but to be able to change the subject so that they aren't embarrassed by what they've asked or what you've said. And it's good again at the right time and in the right place, to have an invitation to those activities of your renewed, lively church that will most appeal to them. Don't just invite them – meet them and bring them, stay with them and find a gentle social occasion later when you can discuss their observations. Don't imagine that their faith-finding depends totally on you. Pray for them and the Lord will use other people and events to lead them on their journey.

Questions for discussion...

When was the last time someone became a Christian in your church?

What help and advice do you need with evangelism?

Should denominations be training more evangelists and less pastors?

About the Authors

Phil Barber is a qualified teacher, lay preacher and successful church planter. For twenty years, he was a senior pastor of Potters Church, Stoke-on-Trent, UK, which the team and himself planted in 1992. He's an ordained minister and canon in the Order of St Leonard. Now retired, he continues to work to help God's Kingdom grow.

Brian Barber began his career as a Religious Education teacher and for many years was a deputy Principal of a Sixth Form College. He is a lay preacher with long involvement in Christian youth work and church planting. Now retired, he's been blessed with a large family and lives in Stoke-on-Trent.

About PublishU

PublishU is transforming the world of publishing.

PublishU has developed a new and unique approach to publishing books, offering a three-step guided journey to becoming a globally published author!

We enable hundreds of people a year to write their book within 100-days, publish their book in 100-days and launch their book over 100-days to impact tens of thousands of people worldwide.

The journey is transformative, one author said,

"I never thought I would be able to write a book, let alone in 100 days... now I'm asking myself what else have I told myself that can't be done that actually can?'"

To find out more visit

www.PublishU.com

Printed in Great Britain
by Amazon